Filipino Americans

Dedication

To my father, Maximo M. Muñoz, who inspired me to climb to greater heights

To: Sis. Maria Grace
1/9/0c
These forces to
you in your ministry
Peace.
Rom Muñoz

Filipino Americans:
Journey from
Invisibility to Empowerment

Romeo S. Muñoz, Ed.D.

Nyala Publishing
Chicago

Nyala Publishing
1250 W. Addison Street
Chicago, Illinois 60613-3840
www.nyalapublishing.com

ISBN 0–9642068–7–0

LC 2002113300

Contents

Acknowledgment   vii
Introduction   ix
Glossary   xii

1 Land of the Morning   **1**
Pearl of the orient   1
    origin of the filipino   4
    legend of ang alamat   5
Regional groups   5
Spanish colonial rule   8
Other settlers   9
Early institutions   10

2 Immigration to the US   **13**
Waves of immigration   13
    first wave   13
    second wave   14
    third wave   16
    fourth wave   17
Invisible presence   18

3 The Interviews   **21**
Preparation   22
Profiles   23
Demographics   27
The questions   29

4 Culture   **33**
Writings and theory   34
    assimilation and acculturation   37

5 Discrimination   **41**
Background   41
Prejudice and discrimination   46

6   Identity   **49**
Worldview   49
Pintig (heartbeat), essence   51
Characteristics   53
    region & dialect   53
    gender   54
Social Structure   55
    marriage   56
    barangay, family   57
    utang na loob, reciprocity   60
    compadrazgo, godfathership   60

7   Family: Center of Change   **65**
Family control vs. individual freedom   66
    individual freedom   68
    school   69
Filipino women in the US   72
Patterns   73
Growing up   75

8   Learning   **81**
Learning style   83

9   Expanding the Filipino Discourse   **93**
Acquired identity   93
Resistance   97
Contradictions   99
A model for visibility   101
Ethnic studies   103
Model minority   105
Changing the future   107

Conclusion   **111**
Notes   **113**
Bibliography   **119**
Index   **128**
About the Author   **130**

Acknowledgments

There are many people I am indebted to who were involved from the inception to the final completion of this magnum opus. Any attempt to create a list of all the people involved with this project would be futile and embarrassing because I cannot remember every one. My deepest gratitude goes to all of them. I know that they personified one of the themes in this study, *utang na loob* (reciprocity), and I will be forever in their debt.

However, there are a handful of persons that I must mention. Foremost are Dr. Paul Ilsley, my professor and mentor and my wife, Soly Muñoz. Paul's guidance and wisdom enabled me to complete this research; Soly's unlimited patience and encouragement, especially when I was tempted to give up, enabled me to "hang on" until the finish line. My deepest gratitude for Paul's belief in me, especially when my faith in myself was at its lowest level. His enthusiasm, meticulous scholarship and unflinching confidence in my abilities were my guiding lights as I traveled through the dark alley in search of the light of intellectual inquiry for truth and freedom.

Dr. Glenn Smith's seminal encouragement to pursue qualitative research using phenomenology as my basis for inquiry was important. He gave me the first push into the critical review of literature on phenomenological methodology.

Special thanks to my late father, Maximo Muñoz, an educator, who gave me the strong motivation to pursue my postgraduate education by constantly reminding me to continue on. I thank my daughters, Cecilia and Ana, for countless hours spent in listening to and transcribing the interview tapes, deciphering my unintelligible handwriting and providing assistance with their computer skills.

And special thanks to the 25 Filipino immigrants, men and women who took time from their busy schedules to openly share their experiences and feelings with me, a stranger. They took me into their homes and into their confidence, allowing me to be a part of their private lives and experiences. In general, Filipinos are hospitable people but in certain ways very private. These individuals not only opened their homes but also bared their hearts, forging mutual respect, friendship and trust between us.

Finally, I want to thank my family who offered continuing loving support, especially my mother Fé, my sisters and my children. They taught me to be patient and stay motivated and focused. One of my sons told me repeatedly, "Dad, since you have gone this far, you have to do it; I think you'd better." Certainly, these words made me think twice about quitting.

Above all, my wife was my constant support and companion and she had to make sacrifices throughout my academic meanderings through the dissertation decathlon and the subsequent crafting of this book. And last, but not least, to all my college cohorts, thank you.

Romeo Solano Muñoz
June, 2002

Introduction

This prophetic message, written in the mid-8th century BCE by the prophet Isaiah tells of the Jewish people in exile who struggled to reach the "Promised Land" promised by Yahweh.

> Be not afraid, I go before you always. Be not afraid, if you pass through the raging water, you shall not drown. Be not afraid, when you walk through the fire, you shall not be burned. I am your God, your savior, and I will give you rest [Isaiah 43:1-3].

The experience of the first Filipinos who migrated to Hawaii mirrors the people of Yahweh. They came to the island of Hawaii as workers on the sugarcane and pineapple plantations, in search of a better life. Their journey into American society, their assimilation, enculturation and empowerment as a people took almost a century to accomplish.

Filipino Americans tells the bittersweet story of the early Filipinos in Hawaii who emerged from the cocoon of invisibility. Like the butterfly, they are soaring into the blue sky of visibility and empowerment in American society.

My personal experience in the beautiful island of Oahu for six weeks in the summer of 2001 confirmed my conceptual understanding gleaned from many books and articles about the experiences of the early migrant Filipinos in Hawaii. Immersed in the heartbeat of the Filipino people in the parish church in Honolulu, I had the happy experience of mingling with the "old timers," the remaining Filipinos who migrated in the early 1900s, who are now in their 80s. One couple for instance, who celebrated their 62nd wedding anniversary, told me the story of their struggles for survival when they came to the islands, described as "paradise" by their recruiters. "Our trust in God guided our life and struggles," they said. At the time, that is what brought Isaiah's words to me.

The book holds a prophetic message about people, uprooted from the comfort of their native Philippines, who came to the "land of promise"—America — in search of a better life. It also gives insight into the experience of the early immigrants, to be conscious of the misconceptions written about them and their mistakes of the past. The book gives credit to the accomplishments of the early immigrant Filipinos, who, because of *hiya* (shame), did not assert themselves to bring their cultural heritage and background to enrich American society. Through hard work and perseverance, the collective experience of these men and women as leaders in their community has been recognized in American society. One of the fastest growing immigrant groups, the Filipino Americans have finally become visible in the economic, social and political life of the mainstream America.

Filipino Americans, vividly traces the rise of a group of people who had been ostracized, as documented by numerous writers and underscored by signs in restaurants and other public areas in California where "dogs are allowed but not the Filipinos." The Filipino immigrants pursued the Promised Land amid struggle and pain; they experienced racism, prejudice and polarization in many strata of American society. Like the *molave*, a tree whose resilience withstands typhoons no matter how strong, the Filipinos rebounded from invisibility to empowerment—economically, socially and politically.

Their struggles have won them success; their humiliation gave rise to recognition in both private and public sectors of American life. The Filipinos have assimilated into the mainstream of American society without losing their unique cultural heritage and values of family, community, hard work and love of God and country.

This book, clearly, is a contribution to the font of knowledge that is much needed in understanding the nuances of people who were once invisible and are now forging ahead in their communities and in their adopted country. This is a valuable resource as sociology as well as history of the Filipino American people — now almost two million strong, the fastest growing Asian immigrant group.

This is also an excellent resource for adult learning and adult education. It demonstrates both the formal and informal learning processes used by adults. The author's deep insight — into the phenomenology of his own life and experience as an immigrant, a student and scholar, in his own right — is an inspiration for budding Filipino scholars who seek a fresh outlook on the integration of fellow immigrants' adult learning and adult experience.

This is also an inspiring depiction of family studies of a different sort, as example of how grandparents and great grandparents are trying to transmit Filipino values and culture to a generation of Filipino immigrants who are searching for their roots and identity. The root of one's culture cannot be transmitted through osmosis; it should be transmitted in both examples, education and *praxis*. This book shows the way and leads the search towards "Filipinoness" — the root of our identity.

Eoli Roselada O.F.M., M.Div.

Glossary

aliping mamamahay slaves in precolonial Philippines

bahala na	"God will provide and He knows what is best for me"
balikbayan	visit back to the Philippines
barangay	extended family group, encompassing the social, economic, political and military units of precolonial Philippine society.
bayanihan	working together in collaboration
compadrazgo	compadre system, alliances based on godparenting
datu	see *Rajah*
encomienda	feudal system
hindi ibang tao	one of us; not a stranger
hiya	wounded pride
ibang-tao	others; strangers
inaanak	godchild
jeepney	Philippine jitney; U.S. Army jeep converted into passenger vehicle
hacienderos	wealthy, landed Philippine elites of Spanish descent
kapwa	implies shared identity (self and other) in Filipino worldview

kalooban	see *loob*
kayabangan	versatility
loob	(*kalooban*) inner self
makibaka	to fight
maynilad	a name derived from the flowering plants, what became the Philippine capital, Manila
merienda	mid-afternoon snack
mestizos	offspring of intermarriages between the indigenous natives and foreigners, such as Spaniards, Americans and other foreign invaders
moros	Moors
ninang	godmother
ninong	godfather
nipa hut	Filipino house made of bamboo and nipa palms
pagkakaisa	unity
pagsasama	cooperation
pagsasamahan	people's cooperative way of living
pakikipagkapwa	see *kapwa*
pakikibagay	cooperation; adapting with
pakikiisa	level of oneness or fusion

pakikisama	level of internalized conformity
pakisama	as a matter of right
pinoys	second generation Filipinos
Rajah	chief (*datu*) of a small kingdom in precolonial Philippines
samahan	togetherness
tabula rasa	blank slate
Taga saan ka, sa atin?	Where did you come from?
taga-ilog, tagalog	river-banks; language spoken by the people of Luzon
tia	aunt
tio	uncle
utang	debt
utang na loob	depth of gratitude toward someone
walang hiya	feeling culpable and mutely outraged

1

Land of the Morning

Pearl of the Orient

The Philippines is one of the largest island groups in the world,[1] sometimes referred to as the "Pearl of the Orient Seas".[2] The Philippine archipelago is composed of 7,107 islands and islets and lies about 1,000 miles off the southeast coast of Asia between Taiwan (Republic of China) and Borneo, and just above the Equator. It is bounded on the west by the South China Seas, on the east by the Pacific Ocean, on the south by the Sulu and Celebes Seas, and on the north by the Bashi Channel. Its strategic location finds the Philippines at the crossroads of international travel lanes. About 2,000 of these islands are inhabited. The biggest islands are Luzon on the north, and Mindanao, Mindoro, Samar, Panay, Cebu, Palawan, Bohol and Masbate on the south. The early Filipino immigrants to the U.S. came from northern

Figure 1. Philippine Topography

Luzon, known as the Ilocos region and from the Visayan Islands on the south.

With a total land area of 115,830 square miles or 300,780 square kilometers,[3] the Philippines is a little larger than the United Kingdom and Ireland, a little smaller than Japan or Spain and about the size of Italy or Arizona. The 11 larger islands take up ninety-six percent (96%) of its total landmass. Luzon (104, 607 square kilometers) and Mindanao (94,532 square kilometers) are the largest islands. In between are the smaller island groups to the south called the Visayas. The whole archipelago is criss-crossed with rivers, streams and mountain ranges of volcanic origin, some of which are still active. The most recent eruption of Mt. Pinatubo in 1991 — a volcano known to be dormant for almost 300 years — proved that.

The most scenic volcano, Mt. Mayon, is cone shaped and erupts every 10 years. This volcano is located near Daraga, Albay where I was born. I experienced one of its furies when I was a teenager, but the eruption was nothing compared to the one that occurred in the 1700s

Figure 2. The Philippine Islands

when an entire town and its population were literally buried in the ashes and lava from the eruption. The church steeple, surrounded by boulders and rocks, is the only part of the building that is still visible — attesting to the eruption's fury and destructive power. Yet Mt. Mayon continues to attract national and international tourists because of its majestic near-perfect cone-shaped outline looming across the blue horizon. It is constantly shrouded by white clouds and bathed by misty rainforests verdant with vegetation throughout the year.

The Philippine climate is tropical and most of the land is fertile. Land crops such as rice, corn and vegetables are cultivated year-round. Seas and freshwater lakes provided most of the early inhabitants with seafood and products for barter. In school, Filipino children learn about their tropical climate and rich natural resources. Filipino heritage, values, customs and mores are handed down by the elders through legend and oral history. By retelling these stories to one another and to their children, the early Filipino immigrants in the U.S. preserved their values, identity and culture.

Origin of the Filipino

The majority of the Philippine population have Malay ancestors somewhat intermingled with Asians and Westerners — such as Chinese, Japanese, Indian, Spanish, American and British. Researchers believe the Malays migrated in large numbers from Malaysia and Indonesia to the islands some 7,000 years ago.[4]

Modern Filipinos belong to eight major ethnolinguistic groups with 87 dialects.[5] The major ethnolinguistic groups are the Tagalogs, the Ilocanos, the Pampangos, the Pangasinans and the Bicolanos in Luzon and the Warrays, the Hiligayons and Sugbuanons in the south or the Visayan Islands. The Muslims in Mindanao have their own language and culture which was added to the major languages because of internal migration.

The mixed-blood inhabitants are known as *mestizos*. They are the offspring of intermarriage between the indigenous natives and foreigners, such as Spaniards, Americans and other foreign invaders. In Filipino society, they are identified by their foreign racial heritage, such as Spanish mestizos, American mestizos, etc. In most Philippine history and literature, the term mestizo refers to Spanish heritage, implying a higher level of social assignment in the community. They are also known as *Spanioles Insulares* or Filipinos. The term "Filipino" is derived from King Felipe II of Spain.

Ferdinand Magellan named the islands he discovered in honor of King Felipe II "Las Islas Filipinas," which was later Anglicized to the Philippine Islands when the U.S. took over the islands from Spain in 1898 under the provision of the Treaty of Paris.

Legend or "alamat" of the First Filipino

Filipinos have their own notions of racial superiority. The color of their skin is explained by a legend told to Filipino children. It goes like this:

> *Once upon a time Bathala [God] created the first humans. God fashioned the first human person in his image from a lump of clay and placed the human figure in an oven. God overestimated the time of baking and the figure came out black. This was the African person.*
>
> *For the second attempt, Bathala was extra cautious and the figure was taken out a little too soon. This was the white person.*
>
> *The third attempt was successful; the figure came out just right — golden brown. Thus, the first brown person came to be and that person is the Filipino.*

In the modern world, especially in the U.S., suntan lotion manufacturers make millions of dollars marketing their products during the summer months to simulate brown skin. Some Filipinos take this as a compliment!

Regional Groups

There are some subtle differences between major (regional) groups of Filipinos in terms of dialect, food, dress, customs and traditions. However, what distinguishes the regional groups of Filipinos most is the language (dialect) they use to identify themselves. For example, people coming from the Tagalog regions speak the Tagalog dialect; from the northern regions of Luzon speak Ilocano, Pangasinan and Pampango dialects and those from the southern regions speak the Bicol and Visayan dialects. There are strong regional-linguistic affinities among Filipinos even in the U.S. where organizations in the urban Filipino centers are based on regional and language affinity and origin.

Aside from language, any major distinction in race, ethnicity or cultural traits disappears. Some contend that distinctions are based on language and culture (lingua-cultural)[6] and others that distinctions are based on geography and economy (geo-economic).[7] Lifestyles do differ between those in the coastal regions who make their living from sea products and commerce and those in the interior who make their living from agriculture and industry. About 40% of this population are urban. Many are college graduates employed in the service or financial sectors. About 60% are rural and make their livelihood from the land. Some remote towns and barrios still have barter economies. Thus, there is a dual economic system and culture.[8]

Before the Spaniards arrived in 1521, an animistic religion predominated the islands. Islam was dominant in the southern part of the Philippines, particularly in Mindanao. Today, about 4% of the population are Muslims — the only group that has resisted foreign cultural or political incursion or domination by Western powers. The Philippine Constitution and laws were passed to recognize Muslim distinctiveness from the rest of the population. Their continued insistence on independent economic, cultural and political institutions constitutes the "Muslim problem" in the nation's body politic.[9]

The northern part of the Philippines, including the Visayan region, was colonized by the Spanish military government with the help of Spanish friars (Augustinian, Franciscans and later, the Society of Jesus or the Jesuits). Two thirds of the Philippines were Christianized under the banner of the Roman Catholic religion. Over 80% of the population is Christian, with 20% comprising various protestant denominations (Aglipayans, the Filipino Independent church, Lutherans, Methodists, etc.).

Most literature on the Philippines — textbooks, encyclopedias, tourist guides, brochures, magazines — describes it as the only "Christian" nation in Asia and the most Westernized.[10] Scholarly and popular debates or forums discussing the racial and cultural composition of the Philippines focus alternately on the nationalist/traditionalist or modern view. One group[11] insists that Filipino culture has been totally Westernized; another group insists that foreign (particularly Western) cultural and institutional incursions have been "Filipinized" or absorbed into the Filipino cultural system.[12] This second notion seems to fit into the current social structures, values and norms of the Filipinos. However, there is almost a universal acceptance of the notion that there is no longer a "pure" native Filipino culture after its "discovery" and colonization by Spain and the United States.

One group, however, has not been tainted by any outside influence: the Tasadays. The Tasadays in the rainforests of Mindanao are considered to be living in the Stone Age and were only located by outsiders in the early 1970s.[13]

Spanish Colonial Rule

The Spaniards, under the leadership of Miguel Lopez de Legazpi, officially took hold of the Philippines in 1565[14] with instructions to colonize the islands, discovered by Ferdinand Magellan in 1521, for the Spanish crown. Legazpi was accompanied by an Augustinian missionary, Fray Andres Urdaneta. Fray Urdaneta also served as his pilot and was a pioneer navigator of the Pacific Ocean.

The conquistador and the missionary embodied the dual character of the colonizer. The sword and the crucifix became the symbol of their conquest of the "indios", a name they coined for the native islanders. Rajah Soliman, the proud warrior and leader of one of the islands repulsed them. Soliman became the first known martyr-hero to die in defense of his homeland. The Spanish soldiers found Soliman's *Maynilad* or *Maynila*— a name derived from local flowering plants — to be a civilized town. This town, Manila, became the Philippine capital.

The Indios were a religious people. They venerated an image or figurine among a huge clump of pandan trees. To this day, this figurine is enshrined in a church in Manila and is known as *la virgin de Ermita*.

Diverse colonial personalities took the stage during this period:

- **Juan Salcedo**, Legazpi's young nephew — the romantic figure who saved Intramuros (a city within-the-walls) from the invading Chinese pirate, Limahong
- **Martin de Tada** — a zealot missionary
- **Governor of Dasmarinas** — the gothic silhouette of a victim of a macabre murder generating in

later years a hunting legend of *la loba negra* (the avenging wife)

- **Morga** — the serio-comic scholar who bungled naval battles but wrote an immortal account of the period

The leading historian and authority on Philippine cartography, Carlos Quirino (with whom I had the opportunity to work in 1967) traces old maps of the Philippines. These, along with early Chinese maps referring to the archipelago, illustrate the Philippines' path through the age of trade and first contact to the era of documentation.

Aside from Morga, other accounts by the Spanish colonizers remain the best sources about how the Filipinos lived during that period. Alzina's descriptions of the Bisaya (written a century later), Juan de Plasencia's accounts and a postwar discovery referred to as the *Boxer's Codex*, which contains not only the written descriptions of 16th century Filipinos, but vivid illustrations as well, all celebrate the introduction of the historian's tool. Customs, beliefs and daily life were diligently recorded in these early chronicles.

Other Settlers

Spanish soldiers and missionaries were not the only strangers in this island archipelago. The Chinese had long established relations with the inhabitants of the Philippines, and some of them lived in the islands. However, they were thought to be *pariahs*. The Japanese too had ongoing contact and a small settlement grew in Manila after the Spaniards came.

And then, there were various unsuccessful intrusions:

- A Chinese adventurer named Feng attempted to found a colony in Manila, only to be repelled by the stronger Spanish soldiers.
- The Chinese pirate, Limahong, also tried to lay waste the "walled-city" (*Intramuros*), but was unsuccessful.
- The Dutch corsairs tried to harass the Spanish galleons. They too, failed to gain entry into the fortified city of Manila.

To this day, the walls (intramuros) stand mighty and proud, keeping would-be invaders out of the city.

Early Institutions

Spanish colonial rule introduced many institutions that became part of the present-day Philippine culture. Christianity obviously became the most important of these. Missionaries were responsible for the brand of Catholicism practiced in the Philippines. A by-product of the Crusades, they viewed Islam — and the Moors who occupied Spain — as an evil competitor. The religious conflict they brought with them has endured. The Spaniards viewed this conflict with the moros as a reconquista: a fight to the death to save the homeland. And Filipino Christianity was that homeland. Stained with this outlook, Filipino Christianity symbolically reenacted the moro wars through moro-moro pageants. The Moros residing in the island of Mindanao did not help matters any with their continual forages and violent incursions into coastal towns throughout the Philippines. The tall, mute watchtowers that dot the coast are living memorials to the cry *"hay moros en la costa"* ("There are Moors on the beach").

The first and most active group of early missionaries was the Augustinians, followed by a long procession of missionaries from different religious orders. There were Franciscan friars, Dominicans, the Company of Jesus (also known as Jesuits) and others.

The printing press ushered in the age of mass media technology rather early — bringing along with it the rough beginnings of an educational system for the children of the elite, the colonizers called Filipinos.

A government system under a governor general appointed by the King of Spain, established to exclusively serve the needs of the Spanish colonies, became a semblance of bureaucratic machinery with its peculiar checks and balances of authority.

Out of a folk adaptation of Christian rituals emerged the social institution called the compadre system or *compadrazgo* (discussed in detail in chapter 6).

Part of the romance of this period is associated with the Galleon Trade, commonly known as the Manila-Acapulco Trade. This romantic vision features sails in the wind, exotic cargoes that made or broke fortunes and piracy and adventure on the high seas. Its economic effect, however, was to inhibit development of internal resources because the colonial government totally engrossed itself in import and export. The age-of-trade contacts with diverse civilizations were thus narrowed down by the Galleon Trade to shipping Chinese silk to Acapulco in return for Mexican silver for China. The galleon link was Acapulco — and this infused a unique Mexican influence into the colonization of the Philippines.

While sweeping changes were taking place in the colonized regions of the Philippines among the Christianized inhabitants, other regions of the archipelago remained as they were or evolved in their own fashion (some developing under the Islamic culture), untouched by the ongoing Westernization process. This included the proud natives known as Tausog and the unique culture of the Ifugao in the northernmost part of the Philippines.

2

Immigration to the U.S.

Waves of Immigration

The Spaniards established the first recorded European settlement in the United States at St. Augustine, Florida in 1565.[15] The first, recorded presence of the Filipinos, known as the "Manilamen" — Filipino crewmembers who deserted the Spanish Galleons and arrived in New Orleans by way of Acapulco and Veracruz, Mexico — was in 1763.[16] However, legal and formal Filipino immigration began after the Treaty of Paris. That is when the United States government acquired the Philippines after the Spanish-American War in 1898, the period of U.S. colonization of the Philippines.

First Wave

The first wave of Filipino immigrants came to the United States by way of Hawaii. They had been recruited as farmhands to work in the Hawaiian sugarcane plantations.

Once on the mainland U.S., these early Filipino Americans worked in orchards, plantations, canneries, kitchens, hotels, ships, bandstands and in other menial jobs.

Second Wave

The first wave of Filipinos immigrants paved the way for the second, from 1906 to 1934. Like the pioneering first-wave immigrants, they found work in fields, orchards, plantations, canneries, etc. Mostly men, they had an honorable work ethic that made them highly sought-after "houseboys" by American families. There were also the pensionados "Filipino scholars" sent by the government to study in U.S. universities but unable to support themselves as full-time students.[17]

Isidro, an immigrant from the second wave, told his story:

I arrived in 1934 aboard the U.S. President Hoover steamboat. My first job was as a farm laborer in Salinas Valley [California]. Every day I was hoeing and cutting 200-yard long vegetable fields in the hot sun from dawn to dusk. I suffered a lot, but the $2 I received for the 10 hours' work was good for me. I was hired because I told them that I would be willing to work even during Christmas holidays.

Juan, another second-wave Filipino immigrant and a chemical engineer, had a different experience. He went to Seattle, Washington. He recounted his first experience:

I arrived in 1934. I knew that life in the United States would be difficult at first, but I felt that it would be successful. I felt happy that I was finally here. Everybody was talking about how great the US is and

I was ready to find out for myself. The buildings were very tall, cars lined the streets and there were so many people. Everything was different and I was looking forward to my future. There was no job for me in Seattle. I took a bus to San Francisco, California, where I have relatives. I lived with my uncle's family in a small two-bedroom house. [This is typical of most Filipinos who came to the U.S. as Immigrants.]

I live by the philosophy I learned from my father: "You live together and help each other out until you can be independent. You lend your help and expect nothing in return. [The Filipino cultural characteristic is called pagtutulungan.] *I worked as a bartender. I learned how to mix drinks. After two months following my arrival, IBM in San Jose hired me. My sacrifice paid off; I was earning $110 a week — compared to $10 a week in the Philippines. I always hear about discrimination, but I have never had any problems with it. I could get along with anybody.*

Unlike first wave Filipino immigrants, Juan had an easier time assimilating into American society. He had a blue-collar job while they had to do menial jobs in the fields or were houseboys. In spite of the second wave's better work opportunities, they still lack recognition, continuing to take a back seat in U.S. corporations.

Benigno was philosophical about it.

I know I had a better education than my supervisors did. I had [a] college degree, my supervisor does not, yet he is over me. I will retire from my job in the same position as I was hired. I do not expect to be promoted. It is the policy of the company. Minorities cannot complain; they just obey. I do not like to rock the boat. I am happy where I am — but I could be happier if I get a higher position.

This is an expression of the *bahala na* characteristic of Filipinos, meaning "Come what may" or "God will provide and He knows what is best for me" Filipinos suffer in silence but with hope in their hearts, hoping things will improve. But they will not take any action that would be perceived as an antagonistic attitude towards authority. This trait seems to have been a result of the Spaniards' long conditioning of Filipino behaviors. Because of strong belief in a Supreme Being who rules every person, they believed they must continue to look up to Him without complaint; otherwise worse things could happen. So, Filipinos continue to work hard and hope that some day things could be better without their doing anything about it.

Third Wave

The third wave started after the Second World War, lasting until 1965. It consisted of the WW II Philippine scouts and war brides. Most had a college education. However, their numbers were limited because of the Tidings-McDuffy Act of 1935, restricting Filipino immigration to the U.S. to 50 people a year.

The 1945 War Brides Act helped these numbers to grow. It allowed Filipino men in the U.S. military to bring their wives and children to the U.S. as nonquota immigrants. Then, in 1946, President Truman signed the

Filipino Naturalization Act, making Filipinos eligible to become U.S. citizens.

Fourth Wave

The Immigration and Naturalization Act of 1965 reopened Filipino immigration allowing a quota of 20,000 immigrants per year and the entry of family members as nonquota immigrants. The Filipino community boomed with the coming of the fourth wave of immigrants. Thousands came during the 1970s and 1980s.

What distinguishes the fourth wave? I believe that because of the differences in education and origin between the "new" Filipino immigrants and their "early" predecessors that their experiences diverge. For example, they would have a different outlook on life, on themselves and on their adopted country.

Because of their education, the later immigrants are better equipped to interact with their new environment — physically, intellectually and professionally. The tensions and difficulties associated with living in a cross-cultural community are mitigated. Because of their skills and training, they have better opportunities in the labor market within the context of free enterprise in the U.S. and the international economy. They did not personally feel the need to culturally or politically align themselves to any host country. They also may have felt that they did not need to assimilate into the American mainstream to attain their economic and professional potential. Unlike their predecessors, they have better options because of the marketability of their skills and training.

Invisible Presence

Filipino Americans are still practically an invisible and silent minority, although they number nearly 2,000,000. As much as their tracks have been blotted out in the sands of time, the Filipinos have been in the United States for a long time. Their genealogy can be traced at least back to the 18th century, when Filipino "slaves" — sailors and fugitives from the Spanish Gallon Trade between the Philippines and Mexico, known as the Manila-Acapulco Galleon Trade — found their way to what is now California and Texas. Later archival documents mention that the Filipinos were dispatched by the French Pirate Jean Laffite to join the forces of Andrew Jackson in the Battle of New Orleans in 1812.[18]

Many Americans, even today, do not recognize a Filipino. Until 1927 or 1928 only a small minority of Americans had become aware that tens of thousands of Filipinos were living in this country.[19] I personally experienced this phenomenon. In 1967, as a graduate student at Eastern Illinois University, I gave a slide-lecture presentation about the Philippines to the Kiwanis Club. After my presentation, a number of people in the group indicated they did not have the slightest idea that the Philippines was once a U.S. territory or colony. Some paraded their ignorance by asking questions such as "Where in the world are the Philippine Islands located?"

For others more informed, the Filipino was born into the American political consciousness when the United States "colonized" a people "sitting in darkness" (as Mark Twain phrased it). The Philippines was colonized under the guise of "benevolent assimilation" — a good intention of then-president McKinley, after the first president of the Philippine Republic, Don Emilio Aguinaldo, surrendered following the Filipino-American War (1899–1902), known as the Insurrection. After colonization, cheap Filipino labor was recruited and transported to the Hawaiian sugarcane and pineapple plantations and farmlands of California on a large scale. This long, weary exodus from the periphery of the island nation to the cities continues with no end in sight. Filipinos are in the U.S. to stay, but somehow it has been and still is a well-kept secret. Although in the majority among Asian-Americans, they are yet an invisible minority in America.

Filipino invisibility has been less a function of numbers than an effect, a symptom of persisting colonial oppression — first by the Spaniards for 400 years, then by the U.S. for about 48 years. No other Asian immigrant group with their thousands of years of culture (in the Filipino case, Buddhist, Confucian and Malay) has endured such subjugation. Filipinos are quick to identify themselves as "Americans" even before formal U.S. citizenship is bestowed.[20] "I even tried to wash out the brown color of my skin because I thought as an American I must be white," a second-generation Filipino American recounted in an interview (a dramatic departure from the "superior" brownness of the *ang alamat* legend).

This book focuses on post-1965 Filipino immigrants and is influenced by concepts, observation and interviews.[21] Of the three major Asian groups in the U.S. — the Chinese, the Filipinos and the Japanese — only the Filipinos came from a colonial experience. From 1898 to 1946, the Philippines was under U.S. sovereignty. In spite of the "special relations" between the Philippines and the U.S. and the popular notion that the Philippines is the most "Westernized and Americanized" nation in Asia, Filipinos have not achieved the social and economic position one would expect. The 2000 U.S. census indicated that, in terms of social and economic position, they ranked the lowest among the three largest Asian immigrant communities.

3

The Interviews

I primarily interviewed post-1965 Filipino immigrants, although I also spoke to a couple of "old timers" — Filipinos whom I chanced to meet at the Filipino National Historical Society's Conference held in Chicago in 1993. These interviewees were fourth-wave Filipinos who came to the U.S. much more prepared professionally due to their Philippine college education and work experience. They immigrated to the U.S. with greater ease and confidence under the provisions of the revised 1965 U.S. Immigration Act. Because of their credentials, education and professions, their group is known as the "brain drain." [22] Studies of Filipino immigration to the U.S. have revolved around the problem of Filipino professionals leaving the Philippines — rather than on their experiences once in the U.S.[23]

Preparation

I examined and reviewed various approaches used in analyzing majority-minority relations in the U.S. in general and the immigration processes and experiences of immigrants in the U.S. in particular. Historical and current data were extensively used to analyze the patterns of Filipino immigration to the U.S. from the turn of the last century (1900) to the present. Historical books written about Philippine immigration to the U.S. between the 1940s and the 1960s were important in understanding issues and perspectives and for looking into the experiences of Filipinos in the U.S.[24]

Data were reviewed from the U.S. Congressional Record, the U.S. Census Bureau, and annual and special reports of the U.S. Immigration and Naturalization Services (INS). The Chicago INS office and the Philippine Consulate General in Chicago provided direct information in response to my specific and direct inquiries about recent Filipino immigrants. These two sources provided data and reports (published and unpublished) from the Philippines.

In addition to professional journals and unpublished technical papers, information was also secured from the popular media both in the U.S. and the Philippines, including publications shut down upon the 1972 imposition of martial law in the Philippines.[25]

The interview results were gathered from one-on-one interviews and self-reflection diary entries. Using a questionnaire, audiotaped interviews focused on demographic and biographic information as well as interviewees' experiences and attitudes about those experiences.

In fact, the interviews were quite therapeutic for me and those interviewed. They spoke quite candidly and felt good after our interview. I was also able to validate my own experiences through them.[26]

Profiles

The population examined consisted of 25 Filipino-American adults from the Midwest, East and West Coast areas in the United States. Their ages ranged from 29 to 75 years of age. Included among the 12 females and 13 males were a cross-section of socioeconomic and educational backgrounds, from postgraduate medical professional educators to a high school diploma holder. The persons described represent 55% of the entire population in the study.

Some interviewees fluently spoke the Filipino (Tagalog) language and all spoke the English language with a variety of accents, depending upon their Philippine regional origin. The two second-generation Filipino Americans stood out in due to their fluent oral usage of the English language. One interesting observation is that 20 out of the 25 respondents were either in the medical field or in some other service-oriented job. Occupations and organizations ranged from postal worker and police officer to physician and educator.

The names of the participants are fictional in order to preserve their anonymity and maintain confidentiality. These names are representative of the population. The pseudonyms accurately reflect the ethnicity of each although a few circumstances have been altered to protect their identities. A random sampling of respondents is presented that typifies the whole group. The persons described below represent the themes I analyze through this book. Because of overlaps of views and responses, I felt it was not necessary to describe each respondent in the study.

Alex Garcia is a 40-year-old lawyer. He came to the U.S. as a student. He is very nationalistic in spite of his long residency in the U.S. He has a private practice and is very active in the community. He is married and has two children.

Pedro Nidea is a 35-year-old single physician. He specializes in radiology. He belongs to a number of Filipino organizations in the Midwest.

Ben Carpio is an accountant. He was self-employed at the time of the interview. He worked with one of the largest electronic companies in the east Coast area for many years. He is a victim of corporate "downsizing" and job relocation. He opted to stay in the area that he is accustomed to but had to sacrifice a lucrative position. He is 55 years old.

Joe Salcedo is another Filipino-American physician, an orthopedic surgeon. He came to the U.S. 20 years ago in order to continue his postgraduate education. Like the many professionals in the medical field, he sacrificed his *amor proprio*, his self-image, when he first came to this country in order to establish his professional integrity and gain the confidence and trust of his fellow physicians. He has a lucrative private clinic in the northwest Indiana area. He is 63 years old and is a proud father of two sons who are also in the medical professions.

A political activist during the Marcos era, **Ramon Ramos** came to the U.S. in order to escape the dictatorial form of government in the Philippines. His thirst to promote peace and justice led him to join a religious order. He is an ordained priest and continues his ministry among Filipinos. He is 46 years old.

Edwina Escaler came to visit her uncle and 30 years later has not returned to the old country. She is a teacher by profession but ended up as an electronic worker in a medical appliance plant. She said that she does not regret being stranded in the U.S. She has visited her relatives in Manila a few times. She considers herself a true Filipino American, but her roots are deeply planted in the Philippines. She is 48 years old and married with no children.

Nena Yabut is also a former teacher. She is one of the post-1965 émigrés, a third-wave immigrant. She works in a local bank. She has held various positions, including clerical, a bank teller, and her present position as an office manager. She is married with three children. She managed to send her children to college. She hopes that in her old age they will take care of her. She believes that the Filipino value of close family solidarity guarantees her security in her later years. She is 56 years old and will continue to work for a few more years.

Myrna Zamora is self-employed as a piano teacher. She tried to work in a structured environment, a parochial school, but found it hard to keep discipline in the classroom. Over 100 youngsters and adults receive her lessons. She enjoys an independent professional life as a teacher. She is 62 and active in the Filipino community.

A historian in his own right, **Pinoy Tan** teaches in a college environment. In his spare time, he tends the rich collection of the Filipino historical documents and artifacts in an East Coast area. Although he is a second-generation Filipino American, he considers himself a true Filipino-Ilocano although he has never visited the Philippines.

Alfonso Madrid is a retired postal worker. He is one of the old timers who came to this country in the early 1900s. He experienced life during the Depression. He is proud to tell stories about the Filipinos who were together during the dark years of the Depression. Their cultural traits of *samahan* and *bayanihan* enabled them to survive the crisis. He is 85 years old.

Juan Turo came to this country by way of Spain. After graduating from the University of Madrid, he decided to pass through the U.S. to visit his sister. Before reaching the state where his sister lives, he ended up in the Midwest. He has been a bilingual coordinator for 22 years. He was forced to retire due to health problems. An educator and a community leader, he organized and led many organizations in the Filipino community. He is 65 years old. His five children are all college graduates and hold important positions in the workplace in the Midwest.

Although she left the teaching profession, she continued her teaching career as a religious leader, a pastor and a caregiver to the poor in the south side of Chicago. Adult learning[27] is personified in Choly Guro. Although she is goal oriented, she is even more learning oriented. Her thirst for knowledge keeps her in the role of a lifelong learner. She is completing a third master's degree, this time in theology, at the age of 60.

If feminism is a virtue, **Cancel Crisostomo** personifies this type. A 38-year-old former religious professional, she worked among the poorest of the poor women in her country and came to the U.S. She decided to change her religious garb to a civilian one and went on to continue her education. After receiving a Masters degree in sociology, she went on to complete a Ph.D. in the same field. Her work to uplift the cause of women's issues makes her a respected Filipino leader in this country. She is in her late 50s and teaches at a Midwestern university.

These respondents ("named" or not) provided all the data for the conclusions of this book. They were randomly selected from an original list of 50 Filipinos in the Midwest and West Coast. Due to geographic difficulties, the final group of 25 was half male (13) and half female (12).

Demographics

The Filipinos who were interviewed came from five (randomly selected) cities, with these characteristics, according to the 2000 census:
- San Jose, California
- San Francisco, California
- Calumet City, Illinois

- Chicago, Illinois
- Seattle, Washington

The 2000 census shows that the concentration of the Filipino population in the U.S. is in San Francisco. Its 2000 population was **46.4%** nonwhite. Of these, **29.1%** were Asian Pacific Islanders (within the Filipinos fall under). By contrast, Chicago's 2000 nonwhite population had about **3.7%** Asian Pacific Islanders (U.S. Bureau of the Census, 2001).

The 2000 U.S. census shows the total U.S. population of **281,421,906** people living in the U.S. of this figure, **35,305,818** people (or **12.5%** of the population) identified themselves of Hispanic origin, who can be of any race. Table 3-1 shows the breakdown by race, while Table 2-1 shows the breakdown of Asians.

The 2000 U.S. Census reported that Filipinos comprised the smallest ethnic/racial group in the U.S. from among the minority groups that were separately counted as racial or ethnic groups. Even so, next to the Mexicans, the Filipinos have been the largest group of immigrants admitted to the U.S. during the last two decades.

Table 3-1. U.S. Population by Race

Race	Population	% of Total Population
White	216,930,975	77.1
Black or African American	36,419,434	12.9
American Indian/Alaska Native	4,119,301	1.5
Asian	11,898,828	3.6
Total:	**281,431,906**	**100.0**

From United States Census of the Population, 2000 by U.S. Bureau of the Census, 2001, Washington DC: U.S. Government Printing Office

The Questions

I opened each interview by asking about why the person had immigrated to the U.S. and why they had chosen to go to a particular locale. I asked them to characterize their perceptions and interpretations of the situations in the Philippines and the U.S.

Respondents' reasons for immigrating to the U.S. complemented their reasons for leaving the Philippines. These reasons fall into two general categories:

- **structural** — forms of government, infrastructure, state of technology, climate, geography, etc.
- **sociocultural**—involving individual and social relationships, including the psychological or social aspects of human experience such as ethnicity, culture values, norms, mores and social relationships and behavior.

The most frequently mentioned concerns were economic: occupational opportunities and job availability.

Table 3-2. U.S. Asian Population

Race	Population	% of Total Population
Asians	10,242,998	3.6
Asian Indian	1,678,765	0.6
Chinese	2,432,585	0.9
Filipino	1,850,314	0.7
Japanese	796,70	0.3
Korean	1,076,872	0.4
Vietnamese	1,122,528	0.4
Other Asian	1,285,234	0.5

From United States Census of the Population, 2000 by U.S. Bureau of the Census, 2001, Washington DC: U.S. Government Printing Office

However, these apparent economic motives connote more than what the term implies under normal conditions.

For example, it is known that four families in the area came from very wealthy families in the Philippines and continue to maintain their high status in their new environment. They are not political refugees. Although they might be making more money here, they actually had a better life in the Philippines in many respects. They had bigger homes in the Philippines; they did not do any housework since they had servants or maids; they did not know how to drive an automobile since the family employed chauffeurs. The family had very high prestige, status and power in the Philippine community which they do not have in the U.S. communities where they now reside.

Interview respondents revealed several reasons for leaving the Philippines. Ramon explained:

In the Philippines, when you become successful and make lots of money, relatives, friends, organizations think you are obligated to help them.

Alfonso elaborated at length:

In the Philippines it is difficult to determine the reasons of your success. Is it on account of your own abilities, or is it because of the help you got along the way? When you are successful, all those who have given you help also think that you owe them something for your success. Of course, we owe them something for what we are [utang na loob]. That is the essence of Filipino life compared to here [pakikisama]. Anyone who can help is obligated to help those who need it.

I do not mind that. But sometimes this obligation is interpreted to mean we have to do what the family wants. We are happy to give our family and relatives anything we have. But just because they help us does not mean they [can] tell us what life to live [walang pakialam].

We really did not intend to stay out of the Philippines indefinitely. In fact, before martial law [September 1972], we could have gone back and had a better life with servants to [do] all the house chores [cooking, laundry, being chauffeured, etc.].

Ben gave his reasons:
My choice was joining the family business or practicing my profession. I wanted to earn a living independent of the family business. The job market in the Philippines for my profession is bad and the pay is low, so I left the country.

Neon explains why she opted to emigrate:
I think I can only stay here for six more years and with God's help, another six in Canada. But I can earn much more during that time than I could in 30 years in the Philippines. I do all kinds of overtime work and substitutions [doing work of colleagues in exchange for the pay] in order to make enough money to take back. When I get back, I can set up a small business that will help my mother and sisters [and] make money for them, and I can practice my profession even if the pay is small.

Another professional, Pablo, from a middle class family in the Philippines gave his reasons for immigrating to the U.S.

It is hard to plan for one's life and your family [wife and children] in the Philippines these days. You also have to consider helping your parents, brothers, sisters and other relatives [damayan] who are less fortunate than you, sometimes at the expense of your own personal advancement. I was making [enough] for me and my children, but not enough to help others in exchange for what others did for me [utang na loob]. So I had to leave to earn more. We had servants and I did not even have to drive our automobile: we also had our own family chauffeur. But from what I read and hear about the Philippines it seems it was good that we left.

Eighteen respondents said that their goals for leaving the Philippines have been realized by leaving the country. The rest of the respondents said that they would have still left the Philippines, even after knowing and experiencing what they now know and feel. Some expressed a desire to return to the Philippines if the economic and political conditions would normalize.

4

Culture

Understanding a nonwhite immigrant group such as the Filipinos requires a conceptual framework from which to view the status of this invisible minority and their relationships within the dominant U.S. society.

The Filipino experience in the U.S. is similar to that of other American immigrant groups in many ways. However, Filipino Americans are also unique due to the relationship between the two nations. Most Filipinos came to America because of a colonial status that enabled them to better their economic life. America continues to offer the dream of a better life to immigrants in spite of the racially based immigration laws which favored European immigrants from the very beginning — although the U.S. has had one of the more liberal immigration policies since 1965.[28]

Writings and Theory

Early studies of Filipino immigrants[29] primarily looked at their experience in terms of structure and function, with little or no historical perspective. Lasker for example wrote the first comprehensive study on Filipino immigration to the U.S. The study included some historical data and pre-immigration characteristics of the Filipino immigrants. Earlier, in the mid-1920s and late 1930, Bogardus[30] produced numerous studies and papers, now obsolete, on various aspects of the Filipino immigrant experience. A 1940 master's thesis by Catapusan[31] looked into the experience of the early Filipino immigrants, the pensionados, government-sponsored scholars. Most of these early works were published in Sociology of Social Research. Although these investigations contributed valuable information on the Filipino immigrants' experience, their analyses were simplistic.

For example, McWilliams'[32] multilevel conflict and change model included pre-immigration history. His work, *Brothers under the Skin*, was particularly interesting because of its insight into majority-minority relations; it examines nonwhite minority groups within the context of race and ethnic relations. His historical perspective examined minority groups as willing and unwilling victims of a capitalist and imperialist structure.

Two outstanding books published in the 1940s — Bulosan's 1943 *America is In the Heart*[33] and Buaken's *I Have Lived with the American People*[34] — are personal, quasi-biographical accounts of the authors' pre-immigration backgrounds. Although these writers came to the U.S. during the same period, they typify two classes of immigrants: Bulosan came from rural peasant origin and Buaken came from the upper-middle professional class. Their themes, however, are similar: the differences between what they were forced to believe (via propaganda) about America and their personal experience with the reality of conditions in America.

In the 1970s, writers used a similar approach. Muñoz, a journalist, tells how Filipinos were making their lives successful in the American system in *Filipinos in America*.[35] He saw the difficulties and hardships Filipinos experienced as due to their prejudicial attitudes towards white Americans. Makibaka[36] (translated literally as "to fight") by Morales uses a conflict-and-change model. Earlier analysis[37] had failed to critically look into the pre-immigration history and experience that could have influenced the Filipino struggle in their new environment.

In the early 1990s, Jamero wrote an article after journeying to his homeland for a one-month visit as a *Balikbayan* (literally meaning "back to our country") after 50 years. He had come to the U.S. as a 4-year-old toddler when his parents immigrated. He sounds a positive note:

> *Almost four years have elapsed since my memorably nostalgic visit to that island nation of my parents...years of hope and fulfillment, both personally and professionally. Within these years however, time to ponder and reflect not only on my experiences per se but also upon how these same experiences relate to the present and future as well as the past. Within this process, gaining valuable understandings and insights into my "roots" and its impact on my self, my identity, my ethnicity and my culture.*[38]

Bulosan was a Filipino immigrant-sojourner, worker and writer in the United States, well aware of the risk of reading into a Filipino identity enveloped in a culture of silence when he wrote *America Is In the Heart*. In his quasi-biographical life history of the whole community of Filipino migrant workers in the U.S., Bulosan invented a metamorphic persona, self-disintegrated by the competitive labor market of the West Coast and Hawaii. In taking his analysis of this split self-image a step further, I can perhaps forge in the process a new Filipino-American vernacular that may restore and energize. Using this new descriptive language, a dialectic of utopian imagination and emancipatory social discipline can extend beyond the boundaries of race, class and gender.

In his early 1930s *Searching the Heart of America*, San Juan eulogizes Carlos Bulosan as a champion for exploring the Filipino identity and self-affirmation "within the political economy of U.S. imperial domination."[39] As stated in an editorial in the *Friends of Filipino People Bulletin*,

> ...it remains exemplary to other people of color claiming their right to be recognized as makers of U.S. history. At the turn of the century, Mark Twain saw the subjugation of the Filipinos — who up to now persist in their refusal to be enslaved, as Bulosan's lifework demonstrates — as the ordeal and crucible of the American republic. This arena of struggle, I submit, may prove decisive in charting the possibilities and fate of the racial democratic transformation of U.S. society in the twenty-first century.[40]

Other non-Filipino researchers and authors on cultural and race issues in the U.S share this sentiment. For example, Bailey-Haynie echoed similar pronouncements when she commented in *The Life-World of African-American Japanese*:

> To engage in serious discussion of race in America, we must begin not with the problems of black people but with the flaws of American society — flaws rooted in historic inequalities and long-standing cultural stereotypes. How we set up the times of discussing racial issues shapes our perception and response to these issues.[41]

Assimilation and Acculturation

The literature on race and ethnic relations has been dominated by the concepts of assimilation and acculturation. *Melting Pot or Not? Debating Cultural Identity* looks into this controversy:

> On the back of every penny, nickel, dime, and quarter, you will find the Latin phrase "E PLURIBUS UNUM," meaning OUT OF MANY, ONE. Many people feel that America is a melting pot, where millions of immigrants from hundreds of countries have come together to become one people with one way of life. Others argue that being an American means that we should recognize and respect our country's many different cultures.[42]

In sociology, assimilation has often been used interchangeably with acculturation. Anthropologists argue that assimilation is only one form of acculturation, with acculturation being defined as a *phenomenon which results when groups of individuals having different cultures come into continuous first-hand contact, with subsequent changes in the original culture of either or both groups.*[43]

and assimilation being defined as

the process or processes by which peoples of diverse racial origins and different cultural heritages, occupying a common territory, achieve a cultural solidarity sufficient at least to attain a national existence.[44]

So, we might define them as merging into the larger group (assimilation) and modifying one's culture because of the larger group (acculturation).

Another view[45] modifies this definition, making a distinction between cultural behavior and social structure. Assimilation is a two-way process involving two or more cultures. It is usually the host culture that erects or opens the barriers that facilitate or limit social participation by the minority groups.

Based on these distinctions, assimilation may be structural or behavioral.[46] Structural refers to the absence of any barriers in all levels of interaction. This is indicated by the absence of any hindrance to intermarriage. Once this level of assimilation is attained, all other forms of assimilation will follow. However, there is a question whether a marriage between persons coming from different races and cultures is a measure of "assimilation," as the term is commonly understood to imply an intergroup phenomenon.

Behavioral assimilation (interchangeable with some definitions of acculturation) perhaps is more applicable to the U.S. The idea implies that minority immigrant groups assume enough of the cultural characteristics and values of the majority to allow them maximum participation in the institutions needed to survive in the host culture.

The Americanization Movement. At the turn of the 20th century until the 1930s, the "Americanization" movement sought to assimilate all Americans, both native and foreign-born, on the Anglo-white majority's terms.

Melting Pot. Later, this concept was replaced by the melting-pot concept — similar to anthropologists' definition of acculturation — in which two or more societies shed parts of their culture and adopt parts of another, resulting in yet a new culture.

Cultural Pluralism. The Canadian experience is used as a model for the concept of cultural pluralism. This is a process by which divergent racial groups adjust to the central institutions of the majority group sufficiently to attain some national stability, while keeping those racial aspects most central to their human and cultural survival. The majority group accepts as given the differences among peoples without denying them their cultural integrity. A major principle of this concept is equality of opportunities in the larger society by all divergent groups.[47]

This idea had been considered earlier in the U.S.:
Did the Germans and Italians of the Lower East Side of New York and the Dutch and English before them, lose a part of themselves to blend into something? Are today's Asians [Filipinos], and Hispanics...and Russians and Arabs, and Haitians—doing the same thing? In other words, has America indeed been a

melting pot? Is it one now? Should it be? Is it better seen as a salad bowl?[48]

These are not idle questions.[49] They have to do with who we are, how we see ourselves as individuals, as Filipinos and what it means to be American. And what are the implications for immigration?

Debates and arguments, pro and con, continue in all segments of the American society, public and private — from the current American Immigration Control Foundation[50] to early questions about threats facing the U.S. from the "Yellow Peril" at the turn of the 20th century:

> *...the government of a nation is confronted with a serious challenge when new entrants [immigrants] become part of one or more political blocks arising not from differences regarding governmental philosophy but merely difference of ethnic origin. The mobilization of ethnic blocs are political conflict groups of the '90s, an era of declining economic expectations will present a government with a growing problem of conflict management.*[51]

5
Discrimination

Background to Discrimination

What is crucial in understanding the Filipino adventure on the North American continent is its departure from the white European immigrant story of success and its affinity with the plight of the Chicanos, Puerto Ricans and other colonized ethnic nationalities. In particular, the U.S. colonial domination of the Philippines from 1898 to 1946 left vestiges of a colonial mindset that would make Filipinos vulnerable to the temptation of the utilitarian ideal.

Unlike the generation of Japanese and Chinese immigrants, Filipinos as a group did not suffer the excruciating humiliation and ordeal of the Exclusion Law and the Yellow Peril. They went straight to the workers' barracks in Hawaii as colonial wards (labeled "nationals"). This ambiguous political position, subordinate to "real" Americans, made their exploitation as contract laborers even rougher.

The U.S. annexed the Philippines through violence. It suppressed the revolutionary forces of the Philippine Republic of General Emilio Aguinaldo who had vanquished Spanish colonialism in the first "Vietnam"—the Filipino-American War of 1899–1902. It is significant that this occurred after the period 1876–1889 when segregation in the American South had just consolidated itself. The war against the Filipino natives was distinctly a racial one. It was carried out under Theodore Roosevelt's slogan of Manifest Destiny, which historically signified white Anglo-Saxon supremacy.[52]

Inspired by social Darwinism, the United States enforced its claim of shouldering the "white man's burden,"[53] its "civilizing mission" in the wake of Reconstruction's failure with military veterans of the Indian Wars and with soldiers and officials from the pacification campaign in Cuba and Puerto Rico.

The current situation of Asian Americans today traces back to a cyclical pattern of recruitment, exploitation and exclusion of Filipinos, Chinese and Japanese immigrants that varied to some extent only based on the power relations between the U.S. and the country of origin. This racial pattern is best understood in light of U.S. territorial expansion in the mid- and late 19th century — after the Mexican War (1845–1848), the Civil War (1861–1865), the closing of the western frontier and subsequent industrial development and crisis, all culminating in the Spanish-American War of 1896. This marked the birth of the United States as an imperial power in the Pacific.

Some divide the imposition of white Anglo-Saxon culture on people of color into two epochs:[54] 1607 to the early 1700s and after the early 1700s. The first period totally excluded nonwhites (blacks and Native Americans) on plantations and reservations. The second period featured segmented, partial, institutional racism. Asians and especially the Chinese were most affected by the transition between the two periods.[55] The Filipino is also sandwiched between the two, as the Filipino was both colonized native and supposed freeworker who could sell his labor but only in a limited way.

Unfortunately, the Filipinos have not been seen in this light. Like other subjugated peoples of color, the Filipino immigrant has been viewed for the most part as a social problem — not yet a model minority. Sociologists claiming expertise in unraveling the text of Filipino ethnicity or identity fault cultural baggage with contributing to the failure of Filipino recruits to adapt to the working conditions in the sugar plantations. They could not stake their claim to the American dream of success:

> For a long time, the young Filipinos (in Hawaii) separated from more militant groups and indoctrinated to submission by the barrio political system known as cacisquismo, made no attempt to rebel against the plantation system. Filipino loyalty to family and region groups has militated against their achieving success in American politics.[56]

Not only is this wrong, but it is simplistic, lacking any historical perspective. From this viewpoint, the rich and dense phenomenology of the Filipino community's suffering and struggle for survival and dignity disappears.

Mainstream social science erases not only this record of victimization, but also the belief that Filipinos can produce changes in their lives, changes which reveal that the Filipino resistance to oppression is part of what has been called the Third World decolonizing process.[57] This resistance against exploitation/racist institutions is clearly revealed in Bulosan's *America is In the Heart*. This narrative also appears in Filipino labor union militancy. This includes the first major interracial strike with Hawaii between January 1920 and April 1924 and the eight-month strike of 31,000 Filipino workers which closed half of Hawaii's sugar plantations. The United Farm Workers of America, which most people think of as a Chicano movement, in fact, was founded after the strike of Filipino farm workers in Delano, California in 1965.

While Filipinos in general became victims of the Anglo-Saxon civilizing mission and its utilitarian ideology in more than a century of colonialism, the centuries-long revolution tradition of the Filipino people remained alive in the popular memory of thousands of farmers who immigrated to Hawaii and the West Coast before World War II. In 1968 a younger generation of Filipino students initiated the formation of Ethnic Studies as a discipline, inspired by tradition to forge an oppositional culture and find increased meaning in their lives.

The culture of the Filipino immigrant, developing in a dependent Third World neocolony, reveals in macrocosm the contradictions between the utilitarian values of transnational capitalism and the tension between personal initiative and collective vision. It reflects the predicament of the Third World native who, despite his/her bondage to the hallucinations of consumerism and materialism nourished by the U.S. mass media, knows that his/her place as an outsider (otherness) is more than society defines. As Franz Fannon writes in *Black Skin, White Masks*, "I am the slave not of the 'idea' but of my own appearance."[58]

The alienation of the "nomad," then, is what draws the Filipino to the U.S. This tantalizing condition seems to be shared by some of the other Asians too, however fragmented their alliances are. What brings them together is the radical challenge they pose to the power bloc that for now defines the dominance of (the questionable) white American identity.

In my interviewees' way of thinking, the U.S. reveals an economy in shambles and a worsening culture — marked by social decay, drugs, alcohol, AIDS, homelessness, organized syndicates and violence — visible everywhere and every day. They see how the need to assert a version of a homogenous American identity is surfacing again. This identity now claims to be based on cultural pluralism and diversity (a rainbow-like coalition). It is a new strategy to manage racial conflicts in the U.S. and in the transnational free enterprise system within the ideal of unity based on adherence to utilitarian liberalism. But as has been observed, "Ethnic pluralism in America has its origin in conquest, slavery, and exploitation of foreign labor."[59] And I agree that this drive to declare a national consensus is based on a continued hierarchy emerging from discussion and negotiated compromise over conflicting interests. This consensus translates into ideology in action. I see here operating a strategy of domination masked by unity. This apparent unity covers up inherent contradictions and conflicting economic and political interests within and between racial, secular or class groupings.[60]

What results is an agreement to values that, in effect, eliminate those cultural and political differences which it claims to be respecting in the first place. At the same time, it rejects the view that inequality is historically and socially constructed.

With this background, is it any wonder that the Filipinos' experience as nonwhites was problematic?

Prejudice and Discrimination

By the 1950s, it was generally accepted that discrimination is the result of prejudice.[61] Among the suggested solutions to the problem was to increase interpersonal communication between races to reduce the occasions that give rise to prejudiced behavior.

In the early 1970s, this view was expanded to distinguish between interpersonal and intergroup relations. Prejudice, in this view, is not the cause but a means used for discrimination.[62] This view was also challenged in McWilliams' *Factories in the Fields* and *Brothers Under the Skin*.[63] He describes how Native Americans, Chinese, Japanese, Indian Hindus, Mexicans and Filipinos were exploited, hired only for menial, low-paying jobs. Despite their low wages, these hardworking immigrants were initially recognized by extolling their virtues. When they were no longer needed, they were perceived as threats in certain economic sectors; they became problems — essentially *persona non grata*. This change caused intense negative stereotyping, creating prejudices and the resulting overt acts of discrimination.

In his study, *Who Needs the Negro,*[64] Wilhelm documents how the intensity of prejudice and discrimination against African Americans varied along with the economic development of the U.S. Some contend that prejudiced behavior is not a product of a prejudiced person, but that it results from the dynamic between an individual's personality and the social environment, that it can be learned.[65] Although others argue that it is, instead, a pathology explaining extreme hostile behavior,[66] this seems an inadequate explanation for what is called the "passive discrimination" of the normal person.

I personally experienced incidents of being discriminated against in the U.S. I have carried the pain of being an immigrant, an Asian Filipino. The color of our skin, our psychological makeup cannot be changed, so the stigma of being a foreigner in this land of diversity will continue to haunt us as long as we live. But, being conscious of the pervasive racism in this country should not deter anyone from achieving his/her human potential. Living our own cultural values, mores, customs and handing them down to our children is a great contribution in forging peace and harmony in a world divided.

6

Identity

Worldview

It would be a challenge for anyone to define universal concepts such as truth, beauty, peace and justice. To attempt to define a worldview is doubly difficult, particularly when dealing with a colonized country and the Eastern Hemisphere. A "Filipino Worldview" is hard to pin down.

Perhaps it is easier to describe a "way of life" — especially when "our way" can be distinguished from "your way". Even defining "national character" is difficult and controversial due to the reluctance to be stereotyped or to be identified with the cultural mainstream, as in the case of immigrants.

In general, worldview is subjective. In other words, what natural (and supernatural) perceptions do people, nations or countries express in their particular religious and secular life? The Filipino worldview, a subjective concept expressed in food, music, radio and television, drama, stories/legends (*alamat*), folk art, fine art and dance.

The socio-psychological term *kapwa* (as in *Kapwa tao*) expresses this worldview. In English, its literal translation would be "other," although its Filipino meaning is altogether different. Kapwa implies recognition of shared identity (kapwa Filipino, kapwa *tao*), for it embraces both the "self" and the "other".

According to Filipino sociologist Hernandez,[67] what a Filipino eats, where the food comes from and how it is prepared and served indicate a relationship between man and nature as intimate as it is practical. Eating is not merely a biological necessity. It is also a social necessity and a socially defined phenomenon of sharing, which brings about friendship and group acceptance. The relationship created when sharing food can involve either *ibang-tao* (other persons like us) or *hindi-ibang tao* (not one of us). Interestingly, the concept of "kapwa" embraces both categories.

In her article on Filipino folk arts and contemporary Filipino painting, Guillermo,[68] stresses the idea that the Filipino worldview is a dynamic, not a static outcome of circumstances and events in which Filipinos cope in the name of "progress". The native arts of the Filipinos — weaving, woodcarving, body decoration (tattoos), architecture, etc. — reflect the interaction between the person (tao) and nature. Other cultural expressions, such as the Filipino house (*nipa hut*) and the *jeepney* (Philippine jitney; U.S. army jeeps converted into public conveyances) express the interaction between the person and the environment.

Filipino religiosity is also manifested in these art forms. Furthermore, these forms express their closeness to nature and openness beyond the cultural phenomenon of kapwa and *pakikisama* (level of internalized conformity).

Pintig (Heartbeat): Essence

Filipino contemporary art's neo-aesthetic approach displays the heights, depths and hardships of the Filipino way of life/worldview. This emerges from *pakikiisa* (level of oneness or fusion), the highest level of kapwa Filipino social psychology.

The year 1905 is significant in the history of the American colonization of the Philippines. It was a time filled with impending changes and rumors of war. In this play within a play, a nationalist theater group bravely sings allegorical stories of love and betrayal to bolster the spirits of Filipinos in the popular movement of the day. Because their future is so insecure, the theater group commits their music and poetry to memory so that their sentiments can continue to live on in the popular imagination.

The Chicago-based Pintig Theater group vividly and artistically portrayed the concept of pakikiisa in *Pintig Scenes from An Unfinished Country 1905/1995*, a recent play. The group, composed of young Filipino American artists in Chicago, attempted to re-stage this seditious play from the turn-of-the-century Philippines. As they unearth fragments of information about the original cast's lives and destinies, they embark on a trip into the history of American colonization and Spanish occupation of the Philippines. They also embark on a journey into their own consciousness as Filipinos — their "filipino-ness" — as they confront issues of identity, race, origin, assimilation, dialogue and change that accompany learning this new culture and adapting to it. This play is the last in a series on Filipino cultural identity, started about the time I began researching and gathering data for this book. A few of the members of this group were my interviewees.

I believe the Filipino worldview is critical to understanding the Filipino American immigrant. In *Reinventing the Filipino: Sense of Being and Becoming*,[69] Azurin examines the discourse of a Filipino scholar reinventing himself. Azurin contends that the Filipino reinvention will be complete once that discourse is conducted in the Filipino language. I agree that the challenge of indigenization of Western concepts, theories and research tools is enormous. There are no English translations of Filipino concepts such as *utang-na-loob*, pakikisama, *hiya* and kapwa. These concepts are reflected upon and debated among social scientists. However, I believe that the levels of social interaction from *pakikitungo* (going along with) to *pagkakaisa*, loob and kapwa must be expressed rather than indigenized.

Filipino immigrants continue to reinvent themselves through learning, both formal and informal. Continuing adult learning provides the venue; self-diagnosis defines learning needs and methods. Life goes on according to one's spirit and inner strength. For the Filipino immigrant, there is a need for moral culture and questioning of the practical: What am I to do? How should I act? How should I change? In the Filipino language/ worldview, it is reduced to "*Papaano ako dapat kumilos*

(How am I to act)?" "*Ano ang dapat kung gawin* (What should I do)?" I address a few of these concerns, especially the challenge of the early waves of Filipino immigrants to emancipate themselves from invisibility.

Characteristics

Although Filipinos often are viewed as a whole, there are some subtle differences between the major groups — in dialect or vernacular, food, customs, dress and traditions. For example, the Tagalogs from Luzon speak the dialect known as Tagalog. The term is literally translated as people from river-banks or *taga-ilog.* The people from the Visayan speak Visayano or Cebuano, etc.

Regions & Dialects

There is a strong regional-linguistic consciousness among the Filipinos. For example, if Filipinos meet in a social setting or in the street, the first question asked is "Where did you come from (*Taga saan ka, sa atin*)?" This is asked to establish the person's dialect and region within the Philippines. When I asked one of my interviewees, Tessie, this question she became excited when she found out that I came from the same province as she did. Her serious demeanor and body language relaxed at once and she became very friendly. We had "connected" and talked about common values, customs, even identified some mutual acquaintances and former classmates from high school. Many organizations in urban centers are based on regional language origins. Just as American students normally identify themselves by race, such as Italian American, Polish American or African American, the Filipinos do similarly by language group or island-regional origins.

Gender

A discussion of the Filipino social structure would be incomplete without mentioning the role and status of women in Philippine society. Filipino women or *Filipinas* have had and continue to have equal status with the Filipino male or *Filipino.* For example, husband and wife can own property in their own name; children can inherit from both directly. In the area of employment as well as participation in economic, political and social activities, women and men have equal status. Not only is there an absence of explicit discrimination against the employment of women in any capacity, but women may even have an advantage over men.

The egalitarian status between the sexes is a long-standing custom. In precolonial Filipino society, women slaves had the same status as male slaves — just as the women in the noble class had the same status as men in that class. In some instances, women even assumed leadership positions in the society.[70] In many instances, the spokesperson of the Tasadays, a Filipino tribe in Mindanao, is a woman.[71] In fact, it has been reported that:

> ...[Filipino] *women before the coming of the Spaniards enjoyed a unique position in society that their descendants during the Spanish occupation did not enjoy. Customary laws gave them the right to be equal to men, for they could own and inherit property, engage in trade and industry and succeed to the chieftainship of the* barangay *in the absence of a male heir. Then, too, they had the exclusive right to give names to their children. As a sign of deep respect,*

the men when accompanying women walked behind them.[72]

Since the Philippines does not have a matriarchal structure, the most viable explanation for the equal status between the sexes is the high value the societies place on the nuclear and extended family. Any family member who is a potential source of status and power for the group will be given recognition, deference, respect and opportunities to develop his/her potential — just as any individual in difficulty can also count on the family or community for support. An example of the latter would be rape, which is not only an assault on a particular woman but is also an affront, a crime against the woman's family and family honor.

Social Structure

The basic unit of Philippine society, the nuclear family, extends to a larger group through affinity and blood relationship. Other networking of the extended family system and larger groups is done through the *compadrazgo*, alliances of families.[73] Philippine social and individual life revolves around the family and the extended group, known as the barangay. The barangay demands an almost absolute loyalty and allegiance throughout a person's lifetime (*pagsasamahan*), so much so that it is almost impossible to observe. For example, conflicts of interest between the individual and the family or group are usually resolved in favor of the latter. The family or group offers material and emotional support and the individual expects it as a matter of right (*pakikisama*). This partially explains why there are very few orphanages for children or nursing homes for older family members, though, of course, poverty does exist among large portions of the Filipino population.

Marriage. The Filipino family extends through marriage. Marriage is not only the union of two individuals, but is also an alliance of families or groups. A family does not "lose" a son or daughter in marriage; rather it gains a son or daughter, including an alliance with another extended family group. In modern Filipino society, prearranged marriages are becoming rare; but young men and women are consciously or subconsciously aware of the boundaries within which to seek marriage partners. Truly, the desire for an absolute "free choice" of a marriage partner is one of the causes of intergroup conflict that individuals often have to confront or overcome. The family does not make absolute demands or narrow the choices; but if the couple expects the support of both families after marriage, they must marry those whom both families can at least "tolerate."

Marital problems can be complex, affecting not only the spouses concerned but the alliance as well. The societal value placed upon marriage and the family is reflected in Filipino society's legal structures through the absence of a divorce law. Until 1972, when the Philippine Congress was dissolved (due to the proclamation of Martial Law by the late President Ferdinand Marcos), the few attempts to legislate or enact some form of divorce law never succeeded.

This does not mean that marriages never break up in Philippine society. While U.S. marriages dissolve in a divorce court, Philippine marriages have other ways in which this can be legally resolved:

- **Annulment** (from bed and board)
  — defines parental obligations and property rights of the estranged parties but does not allow remarriage during the life of one of the spouses.
- **Legal separation**
  — a mutual consent arrangement carrying with it legal sanctions of annulment, such as the one against remarriage.

Moreover, divorces obtained outside the Philippines to dissolve marriages contracted in the Philippines are not recognized.

Family: the barangay. Unions or confederations of families and groups form a larger unit known as the barangay, which encompassed the social, economic, political and military units of precolonial Philippine society. When compared with other countries in the Southeast Asian empires, such as the Siamese kingdoms in what is now Thailand and the Khmer empires known now as Vietnam, Laos and Cambodia, most of what is now the Philippines did not constitute a nation-state or kingdom prior to Spanish colonization.

Barangays or confederations of barangays inhabited the Philippine archipelago. The larger ones were small kingdoms under a chief, known as *datu*, who allied with or was in conflict with other datus. The official title of the chief was Rajah. An example of one such alliance was the one between Rajah Solayman and Rajah Humabon during the time of the discovery of the Philippines by Ferdinand Magellan in 1521.[74]

It is still true that from the nuclear family to the extended family and to the barangay, socialization is oriented towards cooperation and communal welfare rather than toward individualism and individual competition or achievement within the boundaries of family and barangay. It is not that individual effort or achievement is discouraged; rather, achievements are to be shared with the group, just as the group is expected to rally behind the individual in times of need.[75]

The precolonial barangay was a stratified society composed of nobles, warriors, freemen and slaves or *aliping mamamahay.* Power relationships among the classes were paternalistic. Conflicts were with other barangays, not between the classes within the barangays. The Spaniards, and later the Americans, ruled the country through the local established barangays. The Spaniards introduced a plantation type of agriculture where a few Spanish (mostly the friars) and native elites controlled the country's wealth. Until recently, this stratification — with the exception of slavery, which the Spaniards successfully abolished — continued to exist. Although the basis of power and wealth has since shifted from the land (agriculture) to industry, real estate and business, most of the country's wealth remains in the hands of the same powerful families known as the *hacienderos.* During the last 50 years, a middle class has emerged from among the educated professionals such as lawyers, educators, business persons, doctors and nurses and private and government bureaucrats.

Like precolonial society, for the barangay, power is based on factions or alliances of factions that cut vertically across social classes. Once in a position of power, the faction will use the barangay to its advantage to maintain and expand that class position. Maintenance of power is dependent upon the support of the masses (that is, on the peasants, laborers, lower class people, etc.) who traditionally identify with the elites of their own barangay rather than with others of the same lower classes. While the "people power" of the masses was responsible for the overthrow of Marcos's dictatorship in 1986, this structure resembles the traditional feudal system. Although the elite tend to exhibit paternalist concern towards those who serve them, they have and are not averse to using their power to destroy perceived or real disloyalty.

Those in the lower classes believe it is in their interest to identify and form alliances with those in power in the barangay, rather than with those who are similarly situated but who may belong to a different barangay. In practical situations, this means that one's chances of getting "ahead" in society are better if one is allied and identified with power.

The Filipino does not compete as an individual and group interests often supersede individual interests. Instead, Filipinos compete with and among groups, vying for status and power. This conflict and competition for status, sometimes resulting in violence and tragedy, is as continuous as life itself. It penetrates all aspects of Philippine interpersonal and social life.[76]

In addition to intermarriage between groups, among the most often used mechanisms to acquire, expand and maintain group alliances and solidarity are the highly valued norms of *utang na loob* (reciprocity) and *compadrazgo* (godparenthood).

Reciprocity: utang na loob. Loosely translated as "reciprocity," utang na loob is a highly valued social norm. It is a social debt incurred for materials or services received from another. While payment is not always explicitly demanded, it is expected, though not always in the same value or manner in which the *utang* (debt) was incurred. The obligation to repay this debt is not confined to the original parties. For example, repayment may be expected or demanded in the form of support in an interfactional conflict or by voting for the person owed in an election. And debt payment does not eliminate a contractual obligation, it merely transfers the same obligation to the most recent beneficiary of the goods and services. Thus, reciprocal obligations are maintained almost indefinitely.[77]

Godfathership: compadrazgo. Another important social mechanism for expanding kinship and alliances is the compadrazgo system or ritual parenthood.[78] The term "compadre" is derived from the Spanish "padre," meaning father; the feminine form is "madre," meaning mother. The practice originates in Catholic religious rituals introduced by the Spaniards in the Philippines.

As a social system, the spiritual and social bonds forged between a godfather or godmother and the godchild (*ahijado*[a]) date back to when Rajah Humabon was baptized with Ferdinand Magellan, leader of the Spanish Armada that "discovered" the Philippines, as the sponsor or godfather. This complex of social bonding continues to the present. It has become a well-established channel of gaining new political connections or allies and firming up old ones.

Predating Spanish colonization of the Philippines, blood compacts were a common practice between rajahs or native leaders. Such a ritual was performed between Sikatuna (a Filipino leader) and Legazpi (head of the second Spanish Expedition to the Philippines) to seal their friendship. This was done by mixing each other's blood with local coconut wine and each partaking of the mixture as a symbol of friendship and alliance. The compadrazgo system originated in Spain and was spread through the Philippines and South America.[79] This system developed out of the obligation defined by the Catholic Church through the sacraments of baptism, confirmation and matrimony.

According to Catholic Church rules, baptism and confirmation create a spiritual bond between the godfather or godmother and the child. The godfather (or sponsor), as he is called, is given the responsibility of taking care of the child, *in loco parentis*, in the event that the parents are unable to perform their parental obligations. The sponsors in marriage are more properly understood in a social context; they are the official witnesses to the marriage contract and have no obligation to support the newlyweds. These rites, however, generate social relationships and expectations which made the compadre/comadre system part of the Philippine value system. It becomes a debt one owed to another in the social context of utang na loob.

A sponsor in baptism or confirmation establishes a new relationship of co-parenthood. The parents of the child carefully choose the sponsor, usually a person who is known and respected in the community or a relative or an acquaintance of long standing. The sponsor is considered a surrogate parent and is called by a spiritual title by the child: *ninong* for godfather; *ninang* for godmother. The term is translated from the Spanish as *padrino* or *padrina*. Thus, the terms compadre and comadre are derived. The child is called *inaanak* (godchild).

The sponsor is aware of certain obligations to the child, even though the intensity of the relationship between an individual child and their sponsor may vary. Godparents expect to be consulted about or informed of the decisions of consequence affecting the child. If the godparents are childless and wealthy, they may assume financial responsibility for the education of their godchild.[80]

This ritual kin relationship in the compadrazgo system has an integrative social function. It joins economically secure members of the upper class with the economically less secure members of the lower class. In an equally important context, it makes the alliance of socially equal community members emotionally secure and makes intrapersonal communication easier.

One final important consideration of the compadrazgo system has to do with the family's acceptance or preference of the sponsor. The system can be seen to operate mainly to expand the individual's number of extended families (relatives) through ritual means. Some studies have shown that neither the relatives nor non-relatives are favored.[81] Other communities show a definite preference for kin.

As with Western societies, the sociological importance of the compadre system even in the Philippines is likely to diminish with increasing urbanization and industrialization. There is increased emphasis on individualism and the rise of other new forms of social organization. The profound changes that take place as a society develops seem to erode traditional social bonds. One that begins to weaken is the linkage between the individual and kin beyond the immediate family. Hence, a kinship mechanism such as the compadre system may also weaken, though it could be replaced by another in which parents teach their children to consider close family friends as kin.

In summary, Filipinos hold on to their values, even in the U.S. For example, the ability to get along well with others (pakikisama), in particular, is highly valued. Sensitivity to personal affront or self-esteem (*amor proprio*), while not openly expressed as desirable, is nonetheless recognized as the root explanation for approved reactive behavior.

7

Family: Center of Change

Like most people, the Filipinos experience the conflict associated with changes in social structure, values and norms in the surrounding environment. For immigrants, moving to an unfamiliar environment can either magnify or reduce the number or intensity of conflicts. The issues that surfaced most during my interviews included childrearing, divorce, family planning and abortion and the status of women in the U.S.

The traditional Filipino family places major emphasis on

- a strong allegiance to family (nuclear and extended) and
- socialization of succeeding generations to family values and norms.

Today's Filipino parents lament the widening gap between themselves and their children. For these immigrants, generational problems — the generation gap — are compounded by cross-cultural differences.

"I lost control over the discipline of my children," said one Filipino immigrant.

"I am confused [about] what to teach my children about Filipino values and norms of behavior as Filipinos," lamented another.

Common to both are the clash of values, norms and attitudes and the consequent effect on identities and behaviors between the generations.[82] The intensity of the civil rights movement in the 1960s generated interest in the negative effects of race relations on the identities of other non-white minorities.[83] Earlier Asian (Filipino, Chinese and Japanese) immigrants did not have childrearing problems in the U.S. — then again, they were almost all male, alone here without families. Barriers to socializing with the majority (whites), anti-miscegenation laws, religious beliefs, ethnic pride and negative attitudes towards other minority groups prevented them from intermarrying and raising families.[84]

Family Control vs. Individual Freedom

The conflicts encountered by more recent Filipino immigrants raising children in the U.S. were within their own group, as well. Often, problems focus on parental/family control versus the individual freedom idealized by the host (American) society. Thus, their identity problems are transgenerational and interpersonal — as well as cross-cultural.

"My 18-year-old son told me one evening that he was
getting an apartment with a friend,"
confided a mother in the Chicago area.
"I was devastated. I could not believe my ears. My
reaction was to say an emphatic 'no way'."

Filipino families stick together; they are close-knit
and, in the Philippines, live under the same roof until
children marry.
"He moved out in spite of my pleadings,"
she continued as she wiped her tear-filled eyes.
One study of Southern Italian and Eastern European
Jewish immigrants[85] found that (ethnic differences aside)
social class was a major factor in parental control over
children's development and behavior. The study found
that those in the

- **lower classes:** were more permissive of their
  children's age-related activities outside the home,
  but more strict within the home.
- **middle-class:** allowed more autonomy inside the
  home, but exerted more control on activities outside the home.

The Chinese attempted to adopt what they considered the "best of both worlds." They raised their children under the assumption that, as social barriers were
lifted, their children would integrate into the mainstream faster.[86] However, other barriers to integration
and assimilation made the children retreat to their own
ethnic group. This made it easier for parents to train
their children in the values of the old country.

For the Filipino family, conflicts over educating children in a new environment concentrate more on family control: Children must obey their parents. Filipino children accuse their parents of being "antiquated, old-fashioned" and not "in sync" with changing times. Parents, in turn, demand obedience and parental deference and honor without explaining why.

Older immigrants were forced to be content with the racial status quo in order to survive and encouraged children to obey and follow the old country's customs and values. Those children, however, protested these controls because of outside influences and peer pressure.

Individual Freedom

For the newer immigrants, things have changed. The rise of ethnic pride and consciousness of ethnic roots has lessened the challenge of teaching children about their heritage. In the Chicago area, teaching Filipino language and culture has become popular (including classes in the Filipino culture and language that my wife and I started in southeast Chicago).

Most Filipino families express a great deal of anxiety over their inability to rear their children "the Filipino way," pointing to how few relationships their children have with other Filipino children as a major concern. Broad geographic distribution throughout the Chicago area prevents matching of Filipino youth by age or interest. Children's activities outside of school are with their non-Filipino classmates or friends.

"I do not like my children to be 'too Americanized'."
Myrna commented.

"However, I do not discourage them to mingle with other children in the neighborhood. I encourage them to be friends with good American children."

But, indeed, Filipino parents tend to be overprotective.

School

Another major source of anxiety is the school environment. Filipino parents fear that the values of authority and respect for elders will erode. They see future problems for their children because of a materialistic outlook on life, an emphasis on individual rights, an overemphasis on competition instead of cooperation (pagsasama or *pakikibagay*), doing their "own thing" without regard to family honor (premarital sex or [worse] teenage pregnancy).

Some of these are not post-immigration problems since similar problems occur in the Philippines. The difference, however, is the lack of supervision and the extended family support system. Another difference is the financial independence the teenagers have in the U.S.

Trining, a working mother, expressed this concern:
No one can be sure of how our children will grow up. The outside influences are too strong sometimes. In the Philippines, if we cannot control them, we can always depend on a relative. But here we are helpless. We send them to counselors....

Our children think that they are better than us. Just because we are in the U.S. they can earn their own money and do not need us; they do not tell us or ask

*for permission [about] where they go or whom they
are with or if they go out at night, what time they are
[coming] back.*

The problems of raising children resulting from
migration are resolved in favor of what is perceived as
the greater good for the family. Trade-offs have to be
made between the old norms and those required by the
new environment and new social structure.[87]

Juan observed:

*At least the children here can have a few things that
we could not afford to buy for them in the Philippines. In the Philippines, we had to pay for almost
everything with regard to education, such as tuition,
lunch money, bus fare, uniforms, etc. Here almost
everything is free in public schools. Food tickets are
even provided for the poor people on welfare.*

*We thought that it was good to be at a place where
there are Filipino children around. But after hearing
about the Filipino youth gangs in the Bay Area [San
Francisco], we are glad we are not there.*

*After we arrived here [in U.S.], we laid down rules
of behavior. Just because we are no longer in the
Philippines does not mean we will have to abandon
some Filipino customs, values, like respect for parents, etc.*

Filipino parents often rationalized that these problems are offset by the advantages of having their children in the U.S. rather than in the Philippines. They
point out these advantages:

- better education,
- better opportunities for higher education,
- more chances of getting jobs after college and
- improved socioeconomic conditions for both parents and children compared to their counterparts in the Philippines.

I am not attempting to present a complete sociological analysis of the Filipino family; the issues of divorce, family planning and abortion are not fully addressed — except to say that they are not only potential sources of psychological and family conflict but are also one of the cultural challenges of immigration.

Regardless of conflicts over these issues, the Filipino families I interviewed say they try to maintain those traditional values they find most important, while they also tend to change those they consider less relevant to their pursuit of a more meaningful life in their adopted country.

Filipino society places more emphasis on the family as the major determinant of individual and societal survival. Since marriage is the foundation of the family, divorce is therefore a less favorable alternative in resolving marital problems.

Concerning the issue of abortion, most Filipino people are strongly opposed to it. All respondents expressed a commitment to the preservation of life.

Filipinos have, however, a liberal position on family planning (without abortion).[88] Attempts in the Philippines to introduce family planning methods—such methods as abstinence and rhythm—have been gaining wider acceptance.[89]

Filipino Women in the U.S.

Filipinos believe that when a woman achieves a high position in the U.S. — locally, regionally or nationally — that event makes headlines of what would be common events in the Philippines. They also are surprised to observe that women in the U.S., unlike women in the Philippines, seem to lack power within the family, within organizational structures or in the body-politic — something they find surprising in a society known for its individual freedom and equality.

These perceptions are summarized by Jean:

"Here [in the U.S.] it is the man who holds the money and just gives wives the money for household expenses. If the wife works, she spends the money for herself and so do the children who earn [money]. In the Philippines, all the earnings of all the members of the family are handled by the mother for the benefit of the entire family."

One Filipino man said,

"In the Philippines, the wife is the treasurer, auditor, and even the disbursing officer and manager. We did not change when we came [to the U.S.]."

One couple had this to say:

"We do not compete with each other on who is better. Anyone in the family, regardless of sex, who is good and is recognized will bring honor to the family. Once we start competing, we destroy the family and each other."

Most of the respondents are still Filipino oriented and they attempt to maintain the traditional egalitarian status between sexes in their own families.

Patterns

The patterns of the Filipino immigrants in the U.S. are affected by pre-immigration values and norms. Kapwa (among) Filipino are preferred for leisure and recreational activities, although non-Filipinos are not altogether excluded. Relatives (considered part of the family) are the first source for help in time of need. Relationships are maintained through personal correspondence and news sources. These relationships are maintained by sending money to family in the Philippines. Most of the Filipinos I spoke to hoped to retire in the Philippines.

Childrearing in the U.S. brings cross-cultural and inter-generational challenges. Filipinos are conservative concerning issues of abortion and family planning, while liberal on the issue of divorce. Filipinos in the U.S. are trying to maintain the traditional egalitarian status between the sexes within their families. Although Filipino women are still confronted with sex discrimination, as are the rest of American women in the U.S., they are still better off economically and professionally than their counterparts in the Philippines.

Filipino immigrants try to minimize the conflicts between their own values and norms and the structural constraints of the new environment in order to maximize their economic and social participation in the American system. As individuals and as families, they share in the same conflicts that the rest of the American society experiences.[90]

There is some apprehension among Filipino parents about their children being totally acculturated and thus losing their Filipino identity. However, part of this apprehension is simply inter-generational. As regards their culture, there is a conscious or subconscious apprehension about the diminishing control of the family over the individual child. The reasons to leave the Philippines outweighed the anticipated problems associated with child rearing in the U.S.

Trying to maintain Filipino cultural heritage is seen as an individual or family problem. However, openly confronting the racial issue could invite hostilities from certain sectors of the host population, which could hinder their effort to maintain their cultural heritage (not unique to Filipinos). Those traditional cultural values that limit full economic and social participation are redefined or put aside. Those traditional cultural values that provide emotional and psychological security are maintained and remain active in their lives.

Filipino attempts to remain invisible are obvious in their maintaining a low ethnic or racial profile and avoiding association with or participation in racial conflict. This allows them to participate fully in the system while acculturating at their own pace and on their own terms. This invisibility also allows them to maintain their cultural identity without being seen as a threat to the white majority or its institutions. Due to their utang na loob values, Filipinos are grateful for the opportunity to immigrate and make their own way; this overrides the issue of racial discrimination in the U.S. society.

Growing Up in the U.S.

An investigation of the experiences of second-generation Filipino Americans provides a glimpse of what it was like to grow up in this country. A second-generation Filipino American, Pinoy Tan, had this to say:

I was born in Modesto, California, and am a member of the second generation that grew up through the Depression years of the '30s. I attended countless schools while my father followed the crops from camp to camp through central California as a labor contractor or as one of the boys working the fields until we finally settled in Salinas where my father worked for Stolich Farms.

After graduating from Salinas High, I took off for high hopes in San Francisco and when the hopes did not materialize, I left the city for the farmlands in Santa Clara Valley 37 years ago, but became an employee of Santa Clara County. At present, I am secretary for the Santa Clara County Commission on the Status of Women.

When I asked what it was like growing up as a second-generation Filipino American, Nina responded:

This is not a simple question to answer. Before I can think to answer, [a] thousand memories click though my mind like picture slides flashing on a screen at high speed. Only when I force the memories to slow down and pick a scene am I able to give an answer — well, almost. How can you describe in words and feelings that surge through your body when... for example, I remember classroom scenes where all about me...classmates are discussing some great party coming, what they are going to wear, etc. Not once had I even been included in the discussions or invited to those parties, but these classmates were the same ones who would ask my help on some classwork problems or during physical education pick me as a teammate. Oh, they were very friendly and thoughtful towards me...on the school grounds...but walking downtown was a different matter. Some said, "Hello," some passed me by.

Oh, yes, I knew life was tough... I mean, for instance, during summertime, it was awful to have to get up before the sun to go out to the fields to work among cold, wet vegetables. And when the sun came out, sweat dripped in your eyes while belatedly cooling off your body under your sweatshirt and jeans. My brother and I worked to help supplement our parents' earnings and to buy school clothes. It was out in the fields that I learned to pull my mind inward into a hazy dream world away from the reality around us. To this day, I find myself using that escape when the going get tough and I need to replenish my strength.

As to the question of what happened to the strong family ties, the kinship that Filipinos pride themselves on, expressed in words like pagsasamahan, pagkapwa, she responded:

Although we knew about the feelings toward us from the outside world, our parents and tios [uncles] and tias [aunts] made our lives as easy and as comfortable as they possibly could — they shielded us and buffed away the sharp edges. Not until I was on my own did I realize how really life was for such as I and my "camp ghetto" peers, how much of a buffer our parents were between the harsh realities of the outside world and us. Now I think it's time we, the second generation, honor them and show them that their teachings, our heritage and the pride of being Filipinos they instilled in us were not wasted on the wind by proudly passing them on to our children and grandchildren.

I'd like to share with you excerpt from my mother Angie's diary and hope to pass on that pride and heritage to the next generation of Filipino Americans. Mom began her diary on January 10, 1924, seven months short of her 20th birthday. At that time, she had only three years of schooling. Throughout her diary she marveled and expressed joy at being able to read and write, "...to learn my alphabets and to put them together so I can read and write...I am thankful."

It's a priceless family heritage and a small piece of Filipino history [in the United States]. Historical because in writing her life, her peers, those she lived with, her neighbors, her surroundings, she wove in their lifestyle, customs, feelings and mannerisms. She continued her writing on the ship on her way to California, about her steerage companions, the ship plowing though the water and the beautiful sight of a golden dawn and its promises when they entered San Francisco Bay.

*My father's childhood was not a very happy one,
but his fondest memories were of those days in
Manila partly because he was homesick for the Philippines and partly because his struggles for a good
life here were hard. He never talked much about it,
but I guessed how deep his disappointment and
hurts were when he refused to watch Alex Haley's
Roots on TV, saying, "It reminds me too much when
I came here."*

This woman is well educated, yet she confessed
that she encountered discrimination both in the community and in the workplace. She is well accepted as a
professional which helped her to heal the deep wounds
of ostracism and distance she suffered as a second-
generation Filipino growing up in America. She overcame the odds against her to adjust to a new
multicultural environment.

Cordova briefly and beautifully summarizes and adds
to the theme of invisibility experienced not only by the
first-generation immigrants but by second-generation
Filipino-Americans as well:

*We are the forgotten Second Generation, bridging
the past with the present but remaining uncertain of
our future, silent in our thoughts, private in our fears,
deluded within our dreams, hidden in our pursuits,
regretful over our failures, overloaded in our achievements, and omitted by our very own.*[91]

Through their words and documentation — etched
with pride, care and love —will some achievements of
the second generation be recognized. In so doing, all of
us as pinoys (second generation) will not have to be

omitted (invisible) from American society. All of us as Filipino Americans can take pride that our triumphs, no matter how insignificant, are our contribution and part of the larger story of the Filipino-American experience in this country, and inclusion in a true American history. This should be shared with all people, white or black, yellow or brown, in the multicultural society that is America in the 21st century.

Filipinos, like most of the early immigrant minorities, value their roots, their cultural heritage, their Filipinoness, but they do not allow it to be an obstacle in their search for a meaningful life in their adopted country. Someday, they will overcome their invisibility using adult education in the process of acculturation/inculturation.

8
Learning

The concept of learning includes the change and development that occurs in the learner and this is especially pronounced during adulthood. Adult life has been characterized as a time of continual change, not only biologically but intellectually, socially, emotionally and so forth.

Although life tasks and crises provide opportunities for development, they do not guarantee development itself.[92] Although the terms "change" and "development" are not always clearly different, the question here is how much and what kind of change must an immigrant experience to learn and develop?

The first and second waves of the Filipino immigrants were generally recruited from the barrios (villages) of the main island of Luzon. Most, though literate, belonged to the working class in the Filipino society.

They came to the U.S. in search of a better economic life. The third wave of immigrants who came in 1965 was educated; most were in the health professions as doctors, nurses and teachers.

> For immigrants, according to some who study them, *the concept of change also seems integral to conceptualizations of adult learning that range from changes in behavior to changes in internal consciousness. Whether one deliberately or incidentally changes awareness, perceptions, behavior or ways of knowing, learning entails both acquiring the new and letting go of the old.*[93]

Although first applied to the German-American immigrant experience, what has been called informal or working-class education is also relevant to other ethnic groups:

> *...there was a tradition of opposition to established forms of education. Moreover, this opposition was not exclusively limited to educational institutions, but it was understood that education was involved in a much broader cultural ideological struggle.*[94]

Most of the early (pinoy-type) Filipinos were recruited as cheap labor, with a few exceptions. The Philippine government sent some to train in the U.S. as pensionados. But even this group found themselves unable to just pursue their education and they worked as domestic helper or in other low-wage urban service work such as waiter, busboy, cook, gardener, etc.[95]

For these immigrants, change and development had to occur. Their physical and social environment demanded that they reorient their lives—although the development in that situation may have been caused by external changes (events) and vice versa. Perhaps change leads to development—or, instead, development leads to change in nature, modes, interests and content of learning, leading to further development.[96] These patterns seem to apply to the post-1965 immigrants.

Learning Style

Studies in the 1960s found, through interviews, that "continuing learners" fell into three groups:

- **goal oriented** — those who use education as a means of accomplishing clear-cut objectives,
- **activity oriented** — those who take part because they value the activity itself, and
- **learning oriented** — those who seek knowledge for its own sake.[97]

I found that most of the Filipino Americans I interviewed also fell into these categories.

Alex's father sent him to San Francisco during the height of the Marcos dictatorship. His father feared for his life because he was an activist, a student at one of the prestigious universities in Manila.

I did not like to come to the U.S. I had no choice; my father sent me to San Francisco to live with my aunt. I could not continue my political activities directly to overthrow the Marcos government, so I decided to register at San Francisco State. It did not take long to find myself in a leadership role among the Filipino students. I continued my subversive political activities through the student newspaper. I graduated from the law school and passed the law exam and board. I am now a practicing lawyer in San Francisco with specialization in Immigration Law. My education was *sort of forced [on] me; I learned for the sake of learning. I was not a spring chicken you know.*

Joe had a different story. He finished medical school in Manila. He came to the U.S. to pursue advanced studies in his specialization, radiography. He was an intern in one of the hospitals on the north side of Chicago. He had a lucrative medical clinic back home. In Chicago, he had to swallow the bitter pill of being a student again, while the thought of what his colleagues in Manila would think ate at his ego, his sensitivity of hiya and amor propio (Filipino self-image). Because he was goal oriented, he overcame the odds. He relentlessly pursued his goal and was greatly rewarded with a lucrative medical practice in a northwest Indiana hospital.

Other Filipino-American professionals were activity oriented. Jean is an elementary school math teacher. She is a very active woman and prides herself on being a member of a dozen organizations in the Filipino community. She said that she derives a lot of satisfaction from her memberships because she often learns something as a result.

I cannot keep still. My job is okay but I need to do something more. I am involved in the Filipino American Council, the Philippine Educators in America, the local Regional Club, etc. My family doesn't mind. They support my activities, although I have some guilt feelings sometimes when I spend more time outside my home to engage in community activities. But I use these activities as a means to learn and improve myself professionally.

There were other Filipino Americans I interviewed who shared similar learning experiences, which M.S. Knowles dubbed andragogy. He defined it as

...a normal aspect of the process of maturation for a person to move from dependency toward increasing self-directedness, but different rates for different people and in different dimensions of life.[98]

Part of this idea is that people become ready to learn something when they experience a need to learn it in order to cope more satisfyingly with real-life tasks or problems — as in Joe's case. This approach

places a great responsibility on the educator in the adult learning process. He says that the educator has a responsibility to create conditions and provide tools and procedures for helping learners discover their "needs to know."[99]

Jean's story also reveals another dimension of adult learning; the learner sees education as a process of developing increased competence to achieve their full potential in life. They want to be able to apply whatever knowledge and skill they gain today to live more effectively tomorrow.

Basically this adult learning viewpoint depends on four crucial assumptions about the learner's characteristics:[100]

1) As individuals mature, their self-concept changes from dependent toward being self-directed.
2) Adult learners accumulate a growing reservoir of experience that becomes an increasingly rich resource for learning

3) Adult readiness to learn becomes more oriented toward the developmental tasks of their social roles.
4) Time perspective changes from postponing the application of knowledge to immediately applying it and, so, they shift learning style from subject-centered to performance-centered.

A medical surgeon shared his reason for coming to the U.S.:

When I arrived in this country, my fears were confirmed and my hope to learn more was heightened by determination to succeed [at] what I intended to accomplish. My fear of being a laughing stock back in my country if I did not succeed enabled me to pursue my education in the medical field. I was very discouraged when I first came. I was not used to being ordered what to do. I was a practicing physician in the Philippines. Now I had to [take] orders instead of giving them. I think my cultural background both in my family and the expectation of my peers I left behind enabled me to accomplish what I came for. At that time, it was very easy to get an internship in any hospital of your choice. Now it is very hard; it is very competitive. I think it follows the law of supply and demand, even in the medical profession.

To make the story short, I worked at a South Chicago Hospital, first as an orderly, a person transporting patients or helper in the various activities in the hospital. It was tough. I wrote my father about it and he demanded that I go back to the Philippines and begin to practice my profession respectably. My hiya and amor propio *helped me to conquer my feeling of self-pity, discouragement and pressures from my family to go home. I completed my internship within a year and got a respectable job at Cook County Hospital. I went to Wisconsin and now I have been practicing in an Indiana hospital for the past 25 years. I can confidently say that I overcame all odds and accomplished...what I initially came for.*

Others credit adult learning to interaction with the environment.[101] Learning may result from experience and, therefore, may be accidental. Learning in this context is more an attitude than a system; it concentrates more on the learner's need than the institution's convenience; it encourages diversity of individual opportunity rather than a standardized approach:

> *Learning is relatively permanent change in behavior or in behavioral potentiality that results from experience and cannot be attributed to temporary body states such as those induced by illness, fatigue, or drugs.*[102]

Others simply believe that "Learning can be thought of as a process by which behavior changes as a result of experiences."[103]

Conceptually, learning is the process of gaining new knowledge or skills to bring about change in behavior or potential behavior resulting from one's daily experiences. In the case of these early Filipino immigrants, they unconsciously changed their behavior in response to the needs and experiences they encountered in the orchards, vegetable fields, Hawaiian sugarcane

plantations and other places where they were transported to work. Their learning was serendipitous and
informal, outside an institutional setting.[104]

Obviously, school and training environments were
critical to certain types of change and development
(acquiring specific skills, professional credentialing,
etc.). In the case of these immigrants, much of their
learning has been nontraditional.

If their informal learning experiences are to be seen
in a "universal" context, we need to answer these questions:

- What have they learned in their new environ-
  ment?
- Were they aware that learning was taking place?
- How did this nontraditional learning come about?
- Was there a structure or institution that helped
  them learn informally?

In answer, I believe that learning for most Filipino
Americans has been informal and experience-driven
and, for the post-1965 immigrants, formal as well.
They absorbed new cultural experiences from the workplace with limited interaction of other ethnic groups.[105]
Based on the interviews, it appears that the Filipino
Americans learned as a consequence of their own
ethnic backgrounds and prior experiences, coupled
with the experiences in their everyday life. Behavior
change and development were occurring without consciously wanting to change or develop in their new
life. They have used their native language to commu-
nicate with one another at the same time that they
have had to learn the new language of the environment

in order to survive. ESL (English as a Second Language) was not yet the method of instruction; no formal school existed where they could learn the English language. Their oriental tongue had to be forced and reshaped to pronounce the tongue-twisting words of the English vernacular. In essence, their learning was nontraditional education.[106]

The first wave Filipino immigrants, however, did not arrive without any formal schooling. The Spanish friars taught them their prayers from a pamphlet known as *Caton Christiana*. This method of indoctrination into the Catholic religion was done covertly. I went through this process as a child. Before entering the formal school, my brother and sisters were sent to a maestra, a teacher trained by the Spanish friars to teach the *Caton*. We learned to read the alphabets and pronounce the Spanish words; we learned to read and write using Catholic prayers as the model. All prayers had to be memorized and recited orally every day. At home, we did the same. Most of my respondents had similar experiences.

In the new U.S. environment, the Filipino immigrants learned the English language on their own, imitating their American bosses. Using syllabication, they learned to read. Pablo, an old timer who now lives in San Jose, California, recounted his experiences when he first came to this country:

> *I was illiterate in the English vernacular. I [had] learned how to read the* Caton Christina *as taught by the local parish priest in my hometown. I know how to read the alphabets in Spanish, but it was hard for me to translate my knowledge of reading the English alphabets or words. By listening to the [white]*

*Americans, I began to compare the Spanish words
and the English and tried to syllabicate the words and
I was able to read. I taught myself to read this way.*

Filipino Americans learned as a result of both prior
experiences in their homeland and the need to survive
in a new environment. They had no teachers to teach
them the new culture and language. Their instructor
was the lived experience, the harsh reality of surviving
within the currents of discrimination and injustice and
indifference in the workplace.

The first wave Filipino immigrants struggled to survive, especially in California:

• They were literally chased out of town by lynch-
  ing mobs.
• Their sleeping bunkhouses were burned to the
  ground.
• They were jailed for dating white women.

They were even offered the "opportunity" to go back
to the Philippines by the U.S. government who offered
to pay their transportation. The majority refused because
of hiya. They would rather suffer the consequences of
being an immigrant than to face being considered a
failure in their endeavor. In any case, most had nowhere
to go. They had sold everything to come to the U.S.;
they had made a supreme sacrifice to reach their dream
of a better life for themselves and their progeny in this
country.

Thus learning had to take place informally and inci-
dentally in the face of oppression from the white hegemonic society. Their individual struggles have united
them as a people, reminiscent of their barangay in their
hometown. They discovered that the old ways of acting

and behaving had to be modified or transformed.[107] One respondent had this to say:

> I have [had] to learn how to adapt myself in this country, especially in the workplace, as I observe and learn new ways of dealing with situations at work. In the Philippines you cannot talk back to your boss or you get fired. You just have to follow what your supervisor tells you back home. [Here] If you are right and have new ideas you can approach the boss and express your ideas and they welcome them. The reward system for excellent work helped me improve myself. I feel that I am important and my self-image is enhanced. I do not know if this also true in other companies. I appreciate this new learning experience.

This new experience in learning from the environment has been called "purposive learning."[108] It calls into question the assumptions that learning can take place only with specific problem-solving, educational objectives, tasks, etc. and a measurement of same. Adult immigrants have additional needs better met outside formal channels. They need learning that transforms old perspectives into new perspectives on their experience.

9

Expanding the Filipino Discourse

We (and I, inserting myself into this collective proclamation) are still practically an invisible and silent minority! The Filipinos have been here for a long time but the early footprints in the sands of the American shorelines have been overlooked, washed away into oblivion, so we seem invisible.

Acquired Identity

However, our first footprints in the U.S. can be traced all the way back to the 18th century. That was when the Manilamen — Filipino sailors under the Spanish masters and fugitives from the Manila-Acapulco galleons (the commerce between Manila and Spain via Mexico) — found their way to what is now California and Texas. In the dusty archives of Chicago's Newberry Library rare book collection, I found Ayer's *Filipiniana*. Through it I traced the silent presence of hardy Filipino sailor-soldiers who were dispatched by the French pirate Jean Laffite to join the forces of Andrew Jackson in the 1812 Battle of New Orleans.

But it was Philippine colonization by the would-be liberators (the United States military) that paved the way. The ordeal of the Filipino-American War — known as the Insurrection (1899–1902) — and attacks against Don Emilio Aguinaldo when he battled to form the first Philippine Republic (1896) that opened the way for the large-scale transport of cheap Filipino farm laborers to Hawaii and California.

This group was the first wave of Filipino immigrants to the U.S. and they officially set foot on U.S. soil by way of Hawaii.[109] This wave began the weary and tor-turous and seemingly endless exodus of Filipino immi-grants to the U.S. The Filipinos are here, these little brown brothers and sisters, somehow invisible and still a well-kept secret.[110]

Our invisibility has been less a function of numbers than an effect or symptom of persisting colonial oppres-sion, first by the Spaniards, then by the United States. No Asian immigrant cultural group, with their thou-sands of years of Buddhist/Confucian culture, has been subjected to the same. Having lost freedom, Filipinos make up for it by identifying with American ego ideals,[111] from Abraham Lincoln to the most recent rock-and-roll pop celebrity or athletic star. Most Filipi-nos, through satellite consumerism, find themselves at home in a world they have lived in before. This includes not only Hollywood fantasies but the material culture of everyday life — from American English to commercial music to consumer goods of "blue seal" (U.S.-imported) nicotine; from modern nuclear auto guided ballistic missiles, which annihilated both friend and foe alike during the Persian and Middle East Gulf War, to sumptuous *merienda* (a mid afternoon snack) at McDonald's to Avon cosmetics; from condoms to celluloid fantasies of the coveted pot of gold at the end of the rainbow of the American dream.

In 1989, J.T. Hagedorn, a U.S.-born Filipina-American author, wrote *Dogeaters,*[112] providing a new catalog of these symbols, themes and artifacts adapted for survival from the rewritten tablets of an archaic past. When Filipinos encounter rejection or discrimination in the U.S., they are at first puzzled (wounded pride [hiya], feeling culpable and mutely outraged (walang hiya) for not reading the signs correctly in the English vernacular. The psychological reflex (kalooban) is familiar: they promise to prove themselves twice as good as their mentors. Filipinos are in fact known for their versatility in mimicking their adopted American culture.

The modern Filipino is a by-product of the Spaniards, English, Dutch, Chinese, Amerikanos and Japanese, not merely by his/her own will to be recognized, but in language and deeds. Four hundred years of bondage by the Spanish feudal (*encomienda*) system and imprisonment in their own land preceded the famous benevolent assimilation of American instruction.[113] These experiences made the Filipinos a fortunate *tabula rasa,* a blank slate, speaking a language they parrot but do not fully understand, forever subjects and adolescent consumers of the Western culture at the expense of their Oriental one.

The traumatic fixations began in those almost fifty (50) years of indoctrination. First, at the turn of the century, market liberalism and meritocracy etched its signature onto the Filipino psyche. This came in the form of the United States' imposed Manifest Destiny for the people who sit in darkness[114] and the white man's burden of civilizing the barbarian natives into free, English junta.

Admiral Dewey's compadre colonialism and benevolent assimilation command was to "go ashore and start your army." Don Emilio Aguinaldo, the first Filipino president of the Republican Filipinas, was told this as cover to the cunning and real motive of Dewey's agenda — to conquer the island-nation "at all costs."[115] This benevolent assimilation, accompanied by military and economic oppression, ended when formal independence was granted on July 4, 1946. Still, American instruction assumed other forms of high- and low-intensity warfare via "free world enterprise and democracy." It was led by the patron (godfather, the United States of America), over Filipino bodies and souls and threatened by forces of evil (the CIA communist-style communism and Maoism). The Filipino leaders danced gracefully under the pressure of economic reprisal to the music of bahala na mentality.

Long before the Filipino as sojourner, immigrant, pensionado, tourist or political asylum-seeker set foot on American soil, his/her soul, body and sensibility had been prepared by the thoroughly Thomasite (name of the first American teachers) Americanized culture of the homeland. This is particularly true for the indoctrinated second and third waves of Filipino immigrants from 1946 up to the present.[116]

Resistance

I disagree with those who claim that the majority of Filipino immigrants after 1965 carried with them traces of the growing nationalist sentiment in the Philippines before and after the declaration of Martial law by President Ferdinand Marcos in 1972.[117]

The first wave of Filipino immigrants in the late 1800s to the 1920s and 1930s demonstrated a spirit of militant resistance to the political conscience of the popular mass (common tao) period.[118] It was the spirit of Jose Rizal's books *El Filbusterismo* (*The Filibuster*, 1861–1896) and the *Noli Me Tangere* (*Touch Me Not*, 1889–1896) that paved the way for the militancy of the Revolution against Spain and later against the new invader, the Americans (Filipino-American War, 1899–1902).

Popular memory counterpoints the path of migration. Thus with thousands of Filipino workers recruited for Hawaii, about 20,000 of them initiated the first major inter-ethnic strike against the plantation owner on June 19, 1920.[119] The strike lasted for seven months. Again, in April 1924, about 30,000 Filipino workers staged an eight-month-long strike that closed down half of the plantations in Hawaii. During this bloody confrontation, police killed 16 Filipino workers, wounded 4, imprisoned 60 and blacklisted hundreds. Filipinos thus earned the reputation for being dangerous and rebellious workers.[120] These incidents earned them respect paid for in blood, sweat and tears.

Before they were invisible; now their presence as a united group of Filipino people became visible.

With the birth of the United Farm Workers' Union from the historic Delano, California, grape strike of

Filipino workers in September 1965, an era ended. The heroic archetype of Filipino worker[121] is now a nostalgic topic for aging veterans of the class war and their kin in retirement villages and homes. That epoch is now incompatible with the newer genre of forced exile.

The 1898 explosion of revolutionary nationalist passion among the workers, peasants, middle strata and intellectuals has never been replicated — not even by the so called urban insurrection in February 1971 or the People Power uprising in 1986, which overthrew the conjugal Marcos dictatorship. Despite three decades of American indoctrination that converted some into Taft's "little brown sisters and brothers," at least two generations of Filipinos revolted against white, Western domination. Among them were Carlos Bulosan and Manuel Buaken and a host of unnamed, unsung heroes. They came to the U.S. where they had to undergo another apprenticeship of disillusionment:

> *Where is the heart of America: I am one of them, of many thousands of young men born under the American flag, raised as loyal, idealistic Americans under your promise of equality for all, and enticed by the glowing tales of educational opportunities. Once here, we are met by exploiters, shunted into slums (camps), greeted by gamblers and prostitutes; taught only the worst in your civilization (society). America came to us with brightened-winged promises of life, liberty, equality and fraternity — what has become of them?*[122]

Bulosan witnessed the many faces of racist violence at the heart of liberal free-enterprise society. Registering in his sentimental and melodramatic style the fabled shock of recognition, he wrote:

I came to know afterward that in my heart and in many ways it was a crime to be a Filipino in California. I came to know that public streets were not free to my people. We were stopped each time those vigilantes patrolmen saw us driving our car. We were suspect each time we were with white women. It was now the year of great hatred; the lives of Filipinos were cheaper than those dogs.[123]

America Is in the Heart ends with utopian hope. Such a vision is possible only because his testimony of growing up an invisible ethnic pilgrim resonates with the popular memory of folk resistance and numerous peasant uprisings in his hometown in Pangasinan in the Philippines. It is the land of his birth. His roots in the dissident folk tradition and communal life preserved certain cunning in his years of exile, which enabled him to forge the conscience of his race.[124] He developed a cultural consciousness at a time when Filipino guerrillas were fighting the Japanese Imperial Army during the Second World War. Filipino gains, Bulosan discovered in the early 1970s, had again fallen back into invisibility.

Contradictions

Why do I linger on the persisting history of U.S. domination of the Philippines? I dwell on it because it is impossible to understand Filipinos' contradictory behavior without fully understanding the process of subjecting their psyche. Research on structural barriers to social mobility preoccupy graduate students in sociology, anthropology and, in recent years, adult learning. But so far, studies of the Filipino community's historical development in the U.S. have been sketchy, superficial and flawed in their assumptions and conclusions. They rely on the expertise of white male sociologists whose strategy of blaming the victim persists in many textbooks.

The well-known scholar Melendy offers a typical example of this when he speaks about Filipino marginality in his entry on Filipinos in the authoritative *Encyclopedia of American Ethnic Groups.* He begins with a description of origins. Citing the surface details of origins and economics, focusing on the family and kinship structure of the Filipino society, he observes:

> The compadrazgo system required an individual's strong sense of identity with acceptance by the group, and served to promote beliefs that in relationships tolerate no disagreement; that an individual should maintain his proper station in society, not reaching above nor falling below it; and that a person's acts should contribute to his self-esteem but not cause embarrassment to others.[125]

He further reports on the prevalence of gambling as a part of barrio celebrations to show that this inclination prevented Filipino immigrants from saving money despite their diligence. While Melendy alludes to the peculiar status of Filipinos as nationals, neither citizen nor alien, a twilight zone of excluding their naturalization but also preventing their deportation, he does not give this the emphasis it deserves. What is worse is that for Melendy the Filipinos came to the U.S. burdened with values and attitudes (which he considers cultural baggage) that only encouraged prejudice or caused their nonacceptance by the dominant white majority. He also uses this to explain their political nullity as citizens today, hence, their invisibility.

Melendy concluded that the Filipinos, confronted with prejudice both in Hawaii and on the West Coast, divided their world even more sharply than formerly into comrades and enemies. The alliance system that evolved in most California towns was based upon Filipino traditions of reciprocity (bayanihan or utang na loob, hiya, obligations, loyalty and solidarity) and those outside the group were suspect. Filipino loyalty to family and region was an obstacle to achieving success in American politics. There was no clear reason to form a Filipino political organization. Provincial allegiance and personality clashes led the Filipino organizations to multiply rather than to coalesce.

Like a snapshot or painted tableaux, text by this "authority" has frozen thousands of Filipinos inside some hermetically sealed ethnographic museum or time capsule of secular predestination. Unfortunately, this view is still quoted in textbooks of otherwise sophisticated common sense.

As the new century begins, it is time for Filipino American immigrants to this land of milk and honey to turn in a new direction. It is time to change from an invisible to a visible presence in the panorama of American society. I believe that this can be realized with a new way of thinking rising from the ashes of invisibility to the bright light of empowerment.

A Model for Visibility

Today, whenever the notion of American identity is celebrated as a unique composite of European immigrants who passed through Ellis Island, a political decision and a historical judgment are being announced.

A Political Decision is made to represent the others — among others, American Indians, African Americans, Chicanos, Latinos, Puerto Ricans, Asian Americans and a host of peoples of color — as missing or absent from the cultural diversity that makes up this country, the United States of America. Whenever the question of national identity is at stake, boundaries of space and time are drawn.

A Judgment is made to consider others as contained — integrated, assimilated and melted — in the cauldron of the so-called "stew" of cultures in the American society.

Cultural pluralism, one such conventional "self evident" truth, graphically illustrates the melting pot metaphor that homogenizes peoples of color into the white middle class hegemony even as they are simultaneously classified.

> ...today both the Chinese and the Japanese groups rank well above American whites on every measure of socioeconomic status. They are as physically distinctive as their ethnic ancestors — laundry men, "chop suey" restaurants, stoop laborers and railroad builders; but ... are no longer a stigmatized racial minority but a rapidly assimilated ethnic group as evidenced by intermarriage with whites. Who is allowed to enunciate the question of national identity or who can solicit the answer when given a choice; are you an American first and an African American, Asian American, Chicano American,

*Indian American, etc., second or vice versa? Is this a
problem of legitimate representation or ethnic
autonomy? Is it a symptom of the hegemonic sector
of the U.S. society which seeks to speak for the
American nation?* [126]

Clearly, this mapping of territory is a matter of articu-
lating power. As self can only be defined in relation to
the other, this relation has been represented only as
exclusion and inclusion. This occurs despite the contradictory calls made to the idea of "unity in diversity"
(e *pluribus unum*). This slogan, this symbolic umbrella,
is seen to dissolve the demarcation lines of the marginalized, excluded segment of the American society for
the sake of every citizen's liberty and pursuit of happi-
ness, regardless of race, color or creed — "one nation,
indivisible."

Ethnic Studies

In academic circles, especially when the focus is ethnic
studies, the cult of ethnicity is based on the paradigm of
European immigrants' success. The glorification of ethnicity has erased any reference to race and racism as
factors in building the political and economic structures
of the U.S.[127] In the book *Affirmative Discrimination*,
Milton Glazer argues for a return to a laissez-faire political economy at the price of historical amnesia. It has
been seen this way, too:

*[Since the time of Jefferson and Jackson] The United
States had assumed the form of a racially exclusive
democracy — democratic in the sense that it sought
to provide equal opportunities for the pursuit of hap-
piness by the white majority through the enslavement*

of Negroes, extermination of native Indians and territorial expansion largely at the expense of the Mexicans and American Indians.[128]

I suggest that what is needed is research to challenge the standard view of "establishment intellectuals" and federal and state policy. This critique could establish the groundwork for fusing theory and practice in adult education. It would seek to recapture the activist impulse and mobilize the agenda of popular memory by elevating the history of people' struggles to the center of the discipline. This grounding could reshape the intellectual landscape and contribute to empowering oppressed or marginalized groups.

Asian-American studies illustrates the crisis of a discipline[129] born out of the agitation for racial minority access to higher education, the demand for relevant curriculum and the linkage of intellectual pursuits with the needs and aspiration of embattled communities.[130] Its original vision of consciousness raising[131] as part of decolonizing and shaping a new political identity for Asians motivated the questioning of the Euro-centric assumptions. It posed a challenge to dominant thinking of the previous two decades about the nature of social problems, in particular, and the increasing diversity of the Asian-American population, in general. It articulated the shared experiences of Chinese, Japanese and Filipinos that can no longer be applied to Indo-Chinese (Vietnamese and Laotian) refugees.

Considering the drastic change in immigration patterns and the lasting effects of the Reagan-Bush era Asian-American studies (and adult education), one should ask if ethnic studies will continue to conform to the current academic view or will it try to recapture its early vision as part of the wide-ranging popular movements for justice and equality, seeking thorough-going social transformation?

Model Minority

Asian Americans have been homogenized as the model minority and this political position harms them. They are presumed to practice the typical values of individualism, self-reliance, work ethic, discipline and so on. The belief and symbolism of Ellis Island and the puritan heritage in mainstream culture is deeply entrenched in American culture. In light of this, any description of the lifelong learning or struggle of diverse Asian immigrants — especially the Filipino Americans — to resist racist violence and institutionalized discrimination through the "culture of silence" (invisibility) experienced by interviewees may be a disturbing challenge to common sense and popular opinion.

With the sharp decline of middle-class living standards, the cutting of social services and the rollback of the gains of the civil rights movement, many suspect that the myth of the Asian American as a "model minority" was contrived to divide working people, pitting one racial group against the other. During the Reagan era, the mass media lauded their hard work, refusal to depend on welfare and adherence to utilitarian values. It was said, "If the Asians can do it, why can't the Latino Hispanics, Afro-Americans etc.?" The myth of Asian Americans' success may be distorted, offering

ideological affirmation of the American dream in an era anxiously witnessing the decline of the United

States in the international global economy, a collapsing white middle class. [132]

Ignoring the structural problems of society and the economy, this myth provides a "quick-fix" cultural explanation. To make America *numero uno* (number one) in the family of nations, once again, it is necessary to emulate Asians who have accepted the puritan errand into the wilderness, the habit of the heart crystallized in the bedrock values of the hard work, thrift and industry — the utilitarian ethos in which the pursuit of enlightened self-interest is rewarded with material success.

Utilitarianism is the principle that underwrites the model minority myth. It is the logic of competitive or possessive individualism at the heart of market-centered democracy, informing the self-identification of the majority. Asians are the opposite. Utilitarianism functions as the ideology of merit-based competition in the free market economy. Promoted by the mass media and the separation of civil society and the state, utilitarian individualism is essential to producing and reproducing inequality. The ideology runs counter to the *pakikisama-barangay* society of the Filipino Americans.

What are the implications? Victims of Fascist practices are blamed for their failures; nothing is mentioned of structural inequities and the persisting effects of race-oriented legislation. Meanwhile, Afro-Americans and Asians squabble over the control of ghetto grocery stores (dramatized in the 1993 burning of Korean stores in Los Angeles) instead of cooperating to question the fairness of bank lending practices and other unjust institutional practices that breed social decay. The myth not only sanctions deceptively reformist social practices but also denies Asians legal and social protection against institutional discrimination.

Changing the Future

What is the future agenda of research on the Filipino Immigrants? If we, the "others" who are represented by those in power, hope to affirm our fight for self-determination as peoples under God, we need to examine the utilitarian ethic that has become a normal, commonsense part of everyday living.

I view emancipation as requiring a challenge to this ideology. The concept of culture that is assumed within it — while it does seek to reconcile incompatible interests and class and gender differences with the concept of a synthesizing American identity — needs to be negotiated, struggled over.

Cultural pluralism as practiced by the traditional institutions usually includes the concept of dominant and subordinate cultures, whether indigenous or migrant, by promoting a "tolerance" of diverse ethnic practice. This idea needs to be reevaluated with a cross-cultural perspective — both within academic disciplines and in adult education. My concern here is not only to demystify that ideology but also to question its role in making individuals accept their assigned positions in society.

In a consumerist society, spectacle and image exercise decisive power in influencing thoughts and action. Hwang's award winning play *M. Butterfly* has called our attention once again to the damage that demeaning stereotypes can inflict on everyone, in particular on those who hold power. Textbooks and popular mass media tabloids continue to perpetuate the image of Asians — Chinese, Japanese, Indo-Chinese or Filipinos—as the inscrutable Orientals: treacherous, evil and lacking respect for human life. Images of the yellow hordes committing *hara-kiri* or *banzai* attacks found in innumerable films about World War II, the Korean War and the Indo-Chinese (Vietnam) wars help reproduce the now stereotypical but still influential perception of the hyphenated Asian Americans as the degenerate and barbaric "others" who warrant forceful treatment.

What *M. Butterfly*, I think, attempted to demystify is not so much any single media distortion of Asian females as exotic sex objects analogous to Puccini's opera heroines or to any number of Hollywood pot boilers. What it sought to highlight is the process of orientalizing the psychological and philosophical self-awareness that generates the suicidal fantasies of the drama's protagonist M. Gallimarad or any number of rice queens. Hwang confronts the intersection of the myths of racism, sexism and imperialism. It seems to me that we can easily rise above these superficial misperceptions and interact as equal human beings with a gesture of humanistic self-enlightenment. Aside from proclaiming our commitments to truth and ritually examining our consciences, I think what is needed is radical change in the social conditions of everyday life that produce such misperceptions. Only then will the powerfully seductive figure of M. Butterfly become finally resistible.

Meanwhile, in the theater of consumer capitalism, mutations of the stereotype are everywhere. I need only mention how perceptions of Asians as coolie laborers, faceless beasts of burden or docile and subservient workers willing to accept low wages and brutal treat-ment have been replaced by images of Asian whiz kids and aggressive Korean merchants, who have success-fully internalized utilitarianism. These new images are as misleading as *M. Butterfly*'s. The West's projection of the East is of the feminine other asking to be oppressed, victimized and silenced. These images must be seen as a part of the ongoing multilayered discourse about an-tagonisms between cultures.

10

Conclusion

Like most of the immigrants who came in the early 1900s, today's Filipino Americans are occasionally controversial — but they are transforming and constantly improving America. This transformation began soon after World War II and is very much an ongoing phenomenon. The stories of the Filipino Americans are succinctly described in a summary of Ungar's book, *Fresh Blood, New American Immigrants:*

> *an anthology of recent immigrants stories, a collection of individual and group experiences, good and bad, ordinary and profound, realistic and romantic, meant to reveal sides of life in the United States that do not often make it into the news...*[133]

This new Americana is every bit as American as apple pie and bagels and pizza and *lumpia* (eggroll) and *adobo*.

Previous generations of Filipino Americans have long since had their stories recorded and written and enshrined in modern American history. We have a few of them: Bruno Lasker, Carlos Bulosan and others that have told of early tribulations of the early Filipino sojourners, pensionados and plantation workers in Hawaii and the U.S. mainland.

Look beyond appearance and etch out a bit of the surface and you will find that every one of the newcomers has a story to tell that is worth listening to. Unless some of these stories are written and heard, they risk being forgotten and lost, forever.

Empowerment and invisibility are the subjects of this book. Transformation through adult learning and education paved the way for the Filipino Americans to rise from the ashes of invisibility to the new dawn of empowerment. Today, we find Filipino Americans in leadership roles in national and local politics. We have governors, mayors and representatives in local, State and the Federal governments. Physicians and nurses are found in major U.S. hospitals and research institutions. Educators in elementary, secondary and higher learning are equally in positions of leadership.

The individuals and groups I have focused on are not necessarily representative of the total population. They are in fact a macrocosm and an eclectic bunch, chosen randomly because they caught my eye and ear or somehow crossed my path. Admittedly, many have been left out. In the end, the struggles and joys of the Filipino immigrants I met seem to me at least as significant as political polls and economic survey as a means of understanding what is happening and where we, Filipino Americans, are headed.

Notes

1   Zaide, 1987.
2   de la Costa, 1965; Henderson, 1912; Meyer, 1935.
3   Agoncillo, 1972
4   Agoncillo, 1972; Jocano, 1967; Kroeber, 1928; Sawyer, 1900; Zaide, 1987.
5   Fox & Flory, 1974.
6   Fox, 1961, 1963.
7   Pido, 1979; Corpus, 1975.
8   Corpus.
9   Majul, 1973.
10   Pido, 1990.
11   Pido; San Juan, 1986.
12   Pido; San Juan, 1992.
13   Agoncillo & Alfonso, 1960; Corpus; Lance, 1972; MacLaish & Launois, 1972.
14   Werhstedt, 1967; Zaide.
15   Bender, 1992.
16   Crouchet, 1982.
17   Cordova, 1993.
18   Espina, 1988.
19   Lasker, 1931.
20   Goulder, 1971; Hegel, 1972.
21   This study is an investigation using a phenomenology and grounded theory methodology in order to critically look into the Filipino immigrants' experiences in the US.
22   Pido, 1979.
23   Abad, 1974; Aspellira, 1974; Bello & Roldon, 1967; Card, 1974; Cortes, 1969; Gupta, 1973; Jayme, 1971; Keeley, 1972; Parel, 1974; Smith, 1979; Takaki, 1990.
24   In addition to the works of Lasker and McWilliams, other books thoroughly reviews included Grunder and Livezey, The Philippines and the United States, 1951; Agoncillo and Alphonso, History of the Filipino People, 1960; Wolfe, The Little Brown Brothers, 1961; Corpus, The Philippines, 1975; de la Costa, The Jesuits in the Philippines, 1581–1768, 1961; Takaki, The Forgotten Immigrants, 1989; The works of Bogardus, 1929,

1930 and Catapusan, 1940 on the early experiences of Filipino immigrants were also valuable resources.

25   Among these are Time magazine, The New York Times, Newsweek magazine, the Philippine Times (Chicago), Philippine Chronicle (Chicago) and the Balitaan (Los Angeles). The information from the Manila Times and Philippine Free Press provided more recent history and current information. These publications were among those closed down by the Philippines government upon the imposition of martial law in the Philippines in September 1972.

26   Author had access to the Chicago Philippine Consular Office, the Newberry Library in Chicago and numerous university libraries. The author's ethnic background, previous doctoral studies at Southern Illinois University as well as sabbatical from teaching allowed extensive research, wide-reaching contacts within the Filipino community and credibility among the respondents of the study.

27   Knowles, 1980.

28   As reported by the US department of Justice, Immigration and Naturalization Service, 1989.

29   Lasker; McWilliams, 1933; Takaki, 1989.

30   Gogardus, 1929, 1930.

31   Catapusan, 1940.

32   McWilliams, 1964.

33   Bulosan, 1943.

34   Buaken, 1948.

35   Muñoz, 1971.

36   Morales, 1974.

37   Buaken.

38   Jamero, p. 43, 1992.

39   San Juan, p. 2, 1933.

40   Friends of Filipino People Bulletin, p. 17.

41   Bailey-Haynie, p. xii, 1995.

42   Franklin, 1995, p. 5.

43   Redfield, 1939, p. 149.

44   Park, 1949, p. 281.

45   Green, 1947.

46   Gordon, 1964.

47   Ibid.

48 Franklin, 1995, p.8.

49 Opposing Viewpoints, edited by O'Neill (1922).

50 Ibid., p. vii.

51 American Immigration Control Foundation's *America Balkanized* (Nelson, 1994) is an essay in social criticism that contributes to the ongoing debate regarding immigration.

52 Horsman, 1981.

53 McWilliams, 1964

54 Lyman, 1970, pp 156-160.

55 Ibid.

56 Melendy, 1980, p.365.

57 Blauner, 1972.

58 The Filipino rejects the model that Sartre (1948) eloquently formulated in Anti-Semite and Jew and explores instead the line of flight taken by Fannon (1948) in Black Skin, White Masks, premised on a overdetermined otherness, "I am the slave not the 'idea' but of my own appearance" (p.20).

59 Steinberg, 1986, p.5.

60 Casrby, 1980.

61 Adorno, Frenkel-Brunswick, Levinson, and Sanford, 1950.

62 One work supporting this idea was Bernard's The Authoritarian Personality (1971), a socio-psychological study of majority-minority relations.

63 McWilliams, 1939, 1964.

64 Wilhelm, 1970.

65 Raab and Lipset, 1965.

66 Kitano, 1974.

67 Hernandez, 1974.

68 Guillermo, 1966.

69 Azurin, 1933.

70 Blair & Robertson, 1912.

71 Nance, 1975.

72 Agoncillo and Alfonso, 1960, p. 215.

73 Fox, 1961.

74 Agoncillo, 1972.

75 Fox; Jocano, 1967.

76 Hollensteiner, 1963.

77 Hollensteiner; Kaut, 1961.

78 Lynch, 1970.

79   Agoncillo, 1972.
80   According to Fox, a noted anthropologist and social scientist of the Philippine value system
81   Arce and Poblador, 1977.
82   Pido.
83   Erikson, 1966; Fishman, 1981; Poussaint, 1971; Strodtbeck, 1971.
84   Catapusan, 1940; Lasker; McWilliams, 1939; Pido.
85   Psathas, 1957.
86   Hayner and Reynolds, 1937.
87   Pido.
88   Author interviews on Filipino views of family planning support the findings of similar studies conducted both in the US and in the Philippines, specifically Hawlet (1954) and Pido (1979).
89   Flavier, 1970.
90   Comas-Diaz, 1990.
91   Cordova, p. ix , 1983.
92   Basseches, 1984.
93   Boucouvalas and Krupp, 1990.
94   Schied, 1993, p. 61.
95   Lasker.
96   Boucouvalas and Krupp, 1990.
97   Knowles, 1980; Houle, The Inquiring Mind, 1961.
98   Knowles, p.44.
99   Ibid.
100   Hill, 1977.
101   Hermgenhahn, 1980, p.7.
102   Maples and Webster, 1980, p.1.
103   In recent literature, the emphasis has extended beyond formal, deliberate learning to include incidental learning, learning from life experiences through everyday interaction with the environment and with people around them. The proponents of this type of learning include Ingham (1978) and Rossing and Russel (1978). Another related important idea is the notion of tacit, unspoken , untaught learning (Polanyi, 1976). "Most of the practical knowledge adults acquire is tacit "are the findings of Sternberg and Caruso (1985, p. 147). such knowledge is vital to vital to real-world pursuits is argued by Wagner and Sternberg (1985).

104 The concept of prior learning proposed by Mirriam and Cunningham (1990), which involves recognition of the fact that people learn in different ways and places, seems to have been the mode of learning for these people

105 Hartnett (1972) defined nontraditional education as a "set of learning experiences free of time and space limitations" (p.14). Where is the locus of learning? Is the place where one learns important? Is knowledge to be equated with the place where one gets it?

106 According to Cross and Valley (1974), what the learner knows is important, not where she or he gets it.

107 Mesirow, 1981.

108 Mesirow and associates, 1990.

109 Vallangca, 1977.

110 Bulosan; Cordova; McWilliams, 1964; Pido, 1979, 1980; San Juan, 1992.

111 I do not have to review Hegel's phenomenology of the Bondsman and Master to understand why Filipinos are quick to identify themselves as Americans even before the formal bestowal of citizenship.

112 Hagedorn, 1989.

113 Bulosan; McWilliams; Pomeroy, 1993; Steinberg, 1986.

114 Lasker, McWilliams.

115 McWilliams.

116 Bulosan; Pido, 1980; San Juan, 1992

117 Oceana, 1985.

118 Vallangca.

119 Ibid.

120 Ibid.

121 Cushner, 1971; McWilliams.

122 Buaken, 1948, p.20.

123 Bulosan, p.10.

124 Friere uses the phrase "to conscienticize" in his *Pedagogy of the Oppressed,* 1970.

125 Melendy, 1980, p.356.

126 Thernstrom, 1983, p. 55.

127 Glazer, 1975.

128 Saxton, 1977, p.98.

129 Omni, 1988.

130 Ibid.
131 Gramsci, 1971.
132 Takaki, 1989, p. 8.
133 Ungar, 1995.

Bibliography

Abad, R. G. "Migration expectations of Filipino medical graduates: An overview." Paper presented at the Conference in International Migration from the Philippines, East-West Center, Honolulu, HI: 1974, June 10-14.

Adorno, T.W. Frenkel-Brunswick, E., Levinson, D.J., & Sanford, R.N. *The Authoritarian Personality*. Harper and Brothers, New York, 1950.

Agoncillo, T.A. *Philippine History*. Manila, Philippines: Inang Wika, 1972.

Agoncillo, T.A., & Alfonso, O.M. *History of the Filipino People*. Quezxon City, Philippines: Malaya Books, 1960.

Allo, K. *The Cubist Circle*. Riverside, CA: University of California Press, 1976.

Arce, W. F., & Poblador, N.S. "Formal organizations in the Philippines: Motivation, behavior, structure and change." In M. R. Hollensteiner (Ed.), *Society Culture and the Filipino*. Quezon City, Philippines: Institute of Philippine Culture, Ateneo de Manila University, 1977, pp. 43–55.

Aspellira, P. F. *The mobility of Filipino nurses*. Paper presented at the Conference on International Migration from the Philippines East-West Center, Honolulu, HI: 1974, June 10–14.

Azurin, A. M. *Reinventing the Filipino: Sense of Being and Becoming*. Diliman, Quezon City, Philippines: University of the Philippines Press, 1993.

Bailey-Haynie, A. *The Life-world of African American Japanese: An ethno-phenomenological investigation of their learning, meaning, and identity*. Unpublished doctoral dissertation, Northern Illinois University, DeKalb, 1995.

Basseches, M. *Dialectical Thinking and Adult Development*. Norwood, NJ: Ablex Publications, 1984.

Batacan, D. *Looking at Ourselves*. Manila, Philippines: Philaw, 1956.

Bello, W., & Roldon, M.C. *Modernization: Its impact in the Philippines* Quezon City, Philippines: Ateneo de Manila Press (IPC Papers, No. 4), 1967.

Bender, M. *A Resource Guide for Practitioners*. Boston, MA: Singular Publishing, 1992.

Berger, J. *And our faces, my heart, grief as photos*. New York: Pantheon, 1978.

Bernard, J. *The conceptualization of intergroup relations with special reference to conflict*. In G. T. Marx (Ed.), *Racial Conflict: Tension and Change in American Society.* Boston: Little, Brown and Company, 1978, pp. 23–31.

Beyer, H.O. Peabody Museum of Archeology and Ethnology. Cambridge, MA: Harvard University Library Microreproduction Department, 1968.

Blair, E., & Robertson, J.A. (Eds.). *The Philippine Islands, 1898-1912.* New York: Putman's Sons, 1912.

Blauner, R. *Racial oppression in America.* New York: Harper and Row, 1972.

Bogardus, E. "Filipino immigrant problem." *Sociology and Social Research,* 1930, pp. 18, 67–71.

Boucouvalas, M., & Krupp, L. *Adult Education in Greece.* Vancouver: Centre for Continuing Education, University of British Columbia in Co-operation with the international Council for Adult Education, 1990.

Buaken, M. *I Have Lived with the American People.* San Francisco: Caldwell, 1948.

Bulatao, J.A. "Philippines Studies." *Hiya,* 1964 12(3), 424–438.

Bulusan, C. *America is in the Heart.* Seattle, WA: University of Washington Press, 1943.

Carby, H. "Multi-Culture." *Screen Education,* 1980, pp. 34, 62–70.

Card, J.J. "Determinants of the migration intentions of Filipino graduate students in the U.S.A." Paper presented at the Conference on International Migration from the Philippines. East-West Center, Honolulu, HI, 1974.

Catapusan, B.T. *Social adjustment of Filipinos in the United States.* Unpublished doctoral dissertation, University of Southern California, Los Angeles, 1940.

Comas-Diaz, J., & Greene, B. "Women of color: Integrating ethnic and gender identities." New York: Guilford Press. In *Psychotherapy,* 1990, pp. 30–35.

Cordova, F. *Filipinos: Forgotten Asian Americans.* Dubuque, IA: Kendall/Hunt, 1983. A pictorial essay, circa 1763-1963.

Corpus, O. D. *The Philippines* (4th ed.). Englewood Cliffs, NJ: Prentice-Hall, 1975.

Cortes, J. R. *Factors associated with the migration of high-level persons from the Philippines to the U.S.A.* Unpublished doctoral dissertation, Stanford University, 1969.

Costa, H. de la. *Jesuit in the Philippines, 1581–1768.* Cambridge, MA: Harvard University Press, 1961.

Costa, H. de la. *Readings in Philippine History.* Manila, Philippines: Bookmark.

Cross, K.P., & Valley, J.R. "Nontraditional study: An overview." In K. P. Cross & J. R. Valley (Eds.), *Planning Nontraditional Programs.* San Francisco: Jossey-Bass, 1974, pp. 14–20.

Crouchett, L. J. *Vision Toward Tomorrow.* El Cerrito, CA: Downey Place, 1982.

Cushner, N.P. *Spain in the Philippines: From Conquest to Revolution.* Quezon City, Philippines: Ateneo de Manila University, 1971.

Daniels, P.A. *A critical investigation of life in K-Town: Learning to learn the way out of oppression.* Unpublished doctoral dissertation, Northern Illinois University, DeKalb, 1955.

Erickson, E. H. "The concept of identity in race relations: Notes and queries." *Daedalus,* 1966, 94 (1), pp. 145–171.

Espina, M. E. *Filipino in Louisiana.* New Orleans, LA: A. F. Laforde & Sons, 1988.

Fanon, F. *Black Skin, White Masks.* New York: Grove Press, 1948.

Fishman, J.A. "Childhood indoctrination for minority group membership." *Daedalus,* 1981 90 (2), pp. 329–349.

Flavier, J. *Doctor to Barrios.* Quezon City, Philippines: New Day Publishers, 1970.

Fox, R. B. "The Filipino family and kinship." *Philippine Quarterly,* 1961, 2 (1), pp. 6–9.

Fox, R. B. "Men and Women in the Philippines." In B. E. Ward (Ed.), *Women in the New Paris.* United National Educational, Scientific and Cultural organization (UNESCO), Asia: 1963, pp. 342–363.

Fox, R. B. & Flory, E. F. *The Filipino People.* Manila, Philippines: The National Museum and Philippine Coast and Geodetic Survey, 1974.

Franklin, P.A. *Melting Pot or Not?: Debating Cultural Identity.* Springfield, NJ: Enslow, 1955.

Freire, P. *Pedagogy of the Oppressed.* Trans. M. B Ramos. New York: Continuum, 1970.

Friends of the Filipino People Bulletin. Michigan State University Special Collections Division: American Radicalism Vertical File, Lansing, MI, 1977.

Glasser, R., & Strauss, A. *The Discovery of Grounded Theory: Strategies for Qualitiative Research.* New York: Aldine, 1967.

Glazer, N. *Affirmative Discrimination.* New York: Basic Books, 1975.

Goetz, J., & LeCompte, A. *Ethnography and Qualitative Design in Educational Research.* New York: international Publishers, 1984.

Gordon, A. *Assimilation in American Life.* New York: Oxford University Press, 1964.

Goulder, A. W. *The Coming Crisis of Western Sociology.* New York: Avon Books, 1971.

Gramsci, A. *Prison Notebook Selections.* Trans. Hoare, Quntin and Smith. New York: International, 1971.

Gray, F. *Hawaii: The Sugar-Coated Fortress.* New York: Vintage Books, 1973.

Green, A. "A re-examination of the marginal man concept, 1947." *Social Forces,* 26, 1967–1971.

Grunder, G, A., & Livezey, W. E. *The Philippines and the United States.* Norman, OK: University of Oklahoma Press, 1951.

Gupta, M. L. "Outflow of high-level manpower from the Philippines." *International Labor Review,* 1973, 8, pp. 167-191.

Guthrie, G. M., & Bennett, A. B. Jr. *Implicit personality theories of Filipino and Americans.* Unpublished manuscript, Quexon City, Institute of Philippine Culture, Ateneo de Manila, 1970.

Hagedorn, J. T. *Dogeaters.* New York: Pantheon Books, 1989.

Hall, S. "Gramsci's relevance for the study of the race and ethnicity." *Journal of Communication Inquiry,* 1986, 10, pp. 5–27.

Hartnett, D. L. *Introduction to Statistical Methods.* Reading, MA: Addison-Wesley, 1972.

Hawlet, A. *Papers in Demography and Public Administration.* Manila, Philippines: University of the Philippines Press, 1954.

Hayner, N.S., & Reynolds, C. N. "Chinese family life in America." *American Sociological Review,* 1937, 2(5), pp. 630-637.

Hegel, G. W. *The Phenomenology of the Mind.* Toronto, Canada: University of Toronto Press, 1972.

Hermgenhahn, B. R. *An Introduction to Theories of Learning* (3rd ed.). Englewood Cliffs, NJ: Prentice-Hall, 1980.

Hernandez, E. "The Makibaka movement: A Filipino Struggle." Paper presented at the Conference on International Migration from the Philippines, 1974, June 10–14.

Hill, W. F. *Learning: A Survey of Psychological Interpretations* (3rd ed.). New York: Harper and Row, 1977.

Holensteiner, M.R. *Reciprocity in Lowland Philippines: Four Readings on Philippine Values.* Quezon City, Philippines: Ateneo de Manila University, 1963.

Horsman, R. *Race and Manifest Destiny: The Origins of American Racial Anglo-Saxonism.* Cambridge, MA: Harvard University Press, 1981.

Houle, C. O. *The Inquiring Mind.* Norman, OK: University of Oklahoma Press, 1961.

Ingham, R. "Context of learning." In W. Rivera & S. Walker (Eds.), *Lifelong learning Research Conference Proceedings.* College Park, MD: University of Maryland, 1978, pp. 74–82.

Jamero, H. (1992). *Lost Generation: Filipino Journal Vol. 2.* Santa Clara Valley, CA: Filipino Historical Society.

Jayme, J. B. *Demographic and socio-psychological determinants of the migration of Filipinos to the United States.* Unpublished doctoral dissertation, Carnegie-Mellon University, Pittsburgh, 1971.

Jocano, L. F. "Beyer's theory of Filipino prehistory and culture: An alternative approach to the problem." In M. Zamora (Ed.), *Studies in Philippine Anthropology.* Quezon City, Philippines: Phoenix Press, 1967, pp. 10–25.

Juan, I, R. *A Factor Analytic Study of Ability and Personality Tests Currently Used in the Philippines.* Unpublished doctoral dissertation, Loyola University, Chicago, 1976.

Kaut, C. "Utangh Na Loob: A system of contractual obligations among Tagalogs." *Southwestern Journal of Anthropology,* 1961. 17(3), pp. 256–272.

Keeley, C. B. "Philippine migration: Internal movements and emigration to the U.S." *International Migration Review,* 1972, 7, pp. 177-187.

Kerlinger, F. N. *Foundations of Behavioral Research.* Chicago: Holt, Rinehart and Winston, 1986.

Kitano, H. H. *Race Relations.* Englewood Cliffs, NJ: Prentice-Hall, 1974.

Knowles, M. S. *The Modern Practice of Adult Education: From Pedagogy to Andragogy* (Rev. ed.). Chicago: Follett, 1980.

Knowles, M. S. *The Adult Learner: A Neglected Species* (4th. ed.). Houston: TX. Gulf, 1990.

Kovel, J. *White Racism: A Psychohistory.* New York: Columbia University Press, 1984.

Kroeber, A. L. *People of the Philippines.* New York: American Museum of Natural History, 1928.

Lasker, B. *Filipino immigration to the continental United States and to Hawaii.* Chicago: University of Chicago Press, 1931.

Lance, I. *This Too Shall Pass.* Cappagua, NY: Herald Books, 1972.

Lewis, M. *The Carnegies Commission on Higher Education.* Boston, MA: Boston University Press, 1953.

Lewis, M. *The Carnegies Commission on Higher Education.* Boston, MA: Boston University Press, 1985.

Lyman, S. *The Asians in the West.* Reno, NV: University of Nevada Press, 1970.

Lynch, F. *"Social Acceptance Reconsidered."* In F. Lynch & A. de Guzman (Eds.), *Four readings on Philippine values* (3rd ed.) Quezon City, Philippines: (Publisher), 1970, pp. 1–65.

MacLaish, A., & Launois, F. *"Help for the Philippine Tribes in Trouble."* *National Geographic*, 140 (2), 1972, pp. 220–225.

Majul, C. *Muslims in the Philippines.* Quezon City, Philippines: University of the Philippines Press, 1973.

McWilliams, C. *Factories in the Fields.* Boston: Little Brown Book Co., 1939.

Melendy, B. Filipinos. *Encylopedia of American Ethnic Groups.* Cambridge: Harvard University Press, 1980, pp. 35–362.

Mezirow, J. D. "A critical theory of adult learning in education." *Adult Education*, 1981, 32 (1), pp. 3–23.

Mezirow, J. D. *Fostering Critical Reflection in Adulthood: A guide to transformative and emancipatory education.* San Francisco: Jossey-Bass, 1990.

Mirriam, S. B., & Cunningham, P. M. *Handbook of Adult Continuing Education.* San Francisco: Jossey Bass, 1990.

Mirriam, S. B., & Simpson, E. L. *A Guide to Research for Educators and Trainers of Adults.* Malabar, FL: Robert Krieger, 1989.

Morales, R. *Makibaka: The Filipino Americans Struggle.* Los Angeles: Mountainview, 1974.

Muñoz, R. S. *A Study of the Senior Filipino Americans in the Midwest.* Chicago: Filipino American Association, 1971.

Nance, J. *The Gentle Tasadays.* New York: Harcourt, Brace Jovanovich, 1975.

Nelson, B. A. *America Balkanized: Immigration's Challenge to Government.* Monterey, VA: American Immigration Control Foundation, 1994.

Oceana, M. "The Filipino nationalism in the United States: An overview." *Line of March*, Fall 1985, pp. 35–40.

Omni, M. "It just ain't the sixties no more: The contemporary dilemma of Asian American studies." In G. Okihiro et al. (Eds.), *Reflections on Shattered Windows.* Pullman, WA: Washington State University Press, 1977, pp. 50–65.

O'Neill, T. *Immigration: Opposing Viewpoints* (American History Series). San Diego, CA: Greenhaven Press, 1992.

Parel, C. P. *"A survey of foreign-trained professionals in the Philippines."* Paper presented at the Conference on International Migration from the Philippines, Honolulu, HI, 1974, June 10–14.

Park, R. E. *Race and Culture.* New York: The Free Press of Glencoe, 1949.

Pido, A. "A cross-cultural prespective of gender roles: The Case of the Philippines." Paper presented at the North Central Sociological Association Convention, Akron, OH, 1979, April 26–28.

Pido, A. New, "New Immigrants: The Case of the Filipino in Bryce-Laporte." In S. Rey (Ed.), *Sourcebook on the New Immigration.* New York: Center for Migration Studies, 1980, pp. 91–98.

Pido, A. *The Pilipinos in America. Macro/micro dimensions of immigration and integration.* New York: Center for Migration Studies, 1990.

Pomeroy, W. J. *The Philippine colonialism, collaboration, and resistance.* New York: International, 1993.

Poussaint, A. F. "A Negro psychiatrist explains the Negro psychic." In N. R. Yetman & C. H. Steele (Eds.), *Majority-Minority.* Boston: Allyn and Bacon, 1971, pp. 348–358.

Psathas, G. "Ethnicity, social class and parental control." *American Sociological Review*, 1975, 22 (4), pp. 415–423.

Raab, M., & Lipset, T. *The Prejudiced Society.* In G. T. Marx (Eds.), *Racial Conflict.* Boston: Little Brown and Company, 1965, pp. 31–35.

Redfield. R. "The art of social science." *American Journal of Sociology*, 1939, *54*, pp. 181-190.

Rizal, J. *The Subversive (El Filubsterismo).* Trans. L. M. Guerero. London: Longmans, 1961. (Originally published in 1896.)

Rizal, J. *Noli me tangere* (Anthology of ASEAN Literatures Series). Trans. J. Castro. Manila, Philippines: Apo Production Unit, 1989. (Original published in 1896.)

San Juan, E., Jr. *Crisis in the Philippines: The Making of a Revolution.* South Hadley, MA: Bergin and Garvey, 1986.

San Juan, E., Jr." Problem in the Marxist Project of theorizing race." *Rethinking Marxism*, 1989, 2, pp. 58–80.

San Juan, E., Jr. *Writing and National Liberation: Essays in Critical Practice.* Atlantic Highlands, NJ: Humanities Press International, 1992.

San Juan, E., Jr. *Articulations of Power in Ethnic and Racial Studies in the United States.* Atlantic Highlands, NJ: Humanities Press International, 1993.

Sarter, J. P. Anti-Semite and Jew. New York: Schocken Books, 1948.

Saxton, L. *Diversion and Corridor Control System in Western Europe.* Washington: Department of Transportation and Office of Research and Development, 1977.

Schnied, F. M. *Learning in Social Context: Workers and Adult Eduction in Nineteenth Century Chicago.* DeKalb, IL: LEPS Press, Northern Illinois University, 1993.

Shaffir. W., Stabbin, R. A. , & Turowezt, A. *Fieldwork Experience: Qualitative Approaches to Social Research.* Boston: Houghton Mifflin, 1980.

Smith, A. *Nationalism in the Twentieth Century.* New York: New York University Press, 1979.

Spielberg, S. *The Phenomenological Movement: A Historical Introduction.* The Hague: Martin Nijhoff Press, 1982.

Stange, S. *Adult Education and Phenomenological Research: New Directions for Theory, Practice, and Research.* Malabar, FL: Robert E. Krieger, 1987.

Steinberg, D. J. (Ed.). *In Search of Southeast Asia.* Honolulu: University of Hawaii, 1986.

Sternberg, R. J., & Caruso, D. "Practice modes of knowing." in E. Eisner (Ed.), *Learning and Teaching Ways of Knowing.* Chicago: University of Chicago Press, 1985, pp. 143-149.

Strauss, A. L. *Qualitatative Analysis for Social Scientists.* Cambridge: Cambridge University Press, 1987.

Strodtbeck, F. "Family interaction, values and achievement." In N. R. Yetman & C. H. Steele (Eds.), *Majority-Minority.* Boston: Allyn and Bacon, 1971, pp. 305-320.

Takaki, R. *Strangers from Different Shores: A History of Asian/Americans.* Chelsea, Canada: Brown and Company Ltd., 1989.

Takaki, R. *A Different Mirror: A History of Multicultural America.* Chelsea, Canada: Brown and Company Ltd, 1990a.

Takaki, R. *The Forgotten Immigrants.* New York: Chelsea House, 1990.

Thernstrom, S. Ethnic pluralism: "The U.S. model." In C. Fried (Ed.), *Minorities: Community and Identity.* Berlin: Springer-Verlag, 1983, pp. 45–150.

U.S. Bureau of the Census. *Annual Report.* Washington, DC: U.S. Government Printing Office, 1989.

U.S. Bureau of the Census. *Annual Report.* Washington, DC: U.S. Government Printing Office, 2000.

U.S. Bureau of the Census. *United States Census of the Population, 2000.* Washington, DC: U.S. Government Printing Office, 2001.

Ungar Sanford J. *Fresh Blood: The New American Immigration.* New York: Simon and Schuster, 1995.

Vallangca, A. *Pinoy: The First Wave. 1898–1941.* San Francisco: Strawberry Hill Press, 1977.

Wagner, R., & Sternberg, R. J. *Intelligence, Information Processing, and Analogical Reasoning: The Componential Analysis of Human Abilities.* Hillsdale, NJ: Lawrence Erlbaum, 1977.

Werhstedt, F. I. *The Philippine Island World: A Physical, Cultural and Regional Geography.* Berkeley, CA: University of California Press, 1967.

Wilhelm, S. M. *Who Needs the Negro?* New York: Anchor Books, 1970.

Williams, R. *Marxism in Literature.* New York: Oxford University Press, 1977.

Wolfe, L. *The Little Brown Brothers.* Manila, Philippines: Exehwon Press, 1961.

Zaide, G. P. *Philippine History* (9th ed.). Manila, Philippines: The Modern Book Co., 1987.

Index

A
Acapulco, 13
acculturation, 37
adult learning, 52, 87
Aguinaldo, Emilio 17, 42
Augustinians, 8, 10
aliping mamamahay, 58
Americanization movement, 20, 39
andragogy, 85
Anglo-Saxon culture, 43
assimilation, Philippines, 18, 37–38

B
bahala na (Bathala), 16
baranggay, 55, 57–59
benevolent assimilation, 18, 102
blood compact, 61, 67
"brain drain", 21
Buaken, Manuel, 35
Bulosan, Carlos, 34, 98–99

C
California, 19
Catholicism, 10
Catholic Church, 61
Chinese, 9, 67, 104
Christianity, Filipino, 7, 10
Colonial Wards, 41, 47, 62
compadre system, 60–62
compadrazgo system, 62, 100
cultural heritage, 79
cultural value, 74
cultural pluralism, 39, 45, 102

D
discrimination, 41, 46, 73
    pattern of, 42
    passive, 47
diversity, cultural, 45
Dutch, 10

E
empowerment, 101
ethnic pluralism (ethnicity), 45

F
Filipino, Filipina, 4, 54
Filipino origin, 4
    allegiances of, 65, 101
    behavior, 16
    colonial wards, 8,41, 47
    early religion, 6
    identification of, 59
    "invisible" presence in
      America, 18
    legend (alamat), 5
    language and dialects, 6,
      52
    major groups of, 59
    nuclear family, 55, 58
    origin (ancestors), 4
    provincial and regional
    regional-linguistic con-
      sciousness of, 59, 104
    resistance of, 50
    reinvention of, 58
    way of life, 55
    worldview of, 49
Filipino family,
    abortion, 71
    American war (Filipino), 48
    divorce (legal separation),
      62, 63, 71
    early structure, 64, 106
    family, 71
    Filipino-ness, 52
    generation gap, 66, 72–73
    inter-generational
      challenge, 79
    support system, 75

G
Galleon trade (Manila-Acapulco),
    13, 18

H
Hawaii, 41–42
hacienderos, 58
hegemony, 102

128

hiya, 101, 58 (*see walang hiya*)

I

immigration,
  classes of, 19–24
  first wave, 13, 100
  second wave, 14
  third wave, 16
  fourth wave, 17, 31–32,
    37–38

J

Jackson, Andrew, 103
Japanese, 10, 19, 102, 104
Jesuits, 7, 11

K

kalooban, 101 (*see loob*)
kapwa, 50
kinship, 6, 100
Knowles, M.S., 124

L

legend (alamat), 5
loob 37, 60, 65, 66, 74

M

Magellan, Ferdinand, 5
Manila-Acapulco trade, 13
mestizo,
  American, 4
  Spanish (Filipino insulares),
    4
  moros (Moors), 10
  muslim, 7

P

pagkapuwa (*see* kapwa)
pensionados, 14
Philippines, 1–3

Q

Quirino, Carlos (Filipino
  historian), 9

R

racial discrimination, 74
Roosevelt, Theodore, 42

S

Spanish American War, 42
Spanish galleon trade (*see Manila-
  Acapulco trade*)
Spanish Rule, 8

T

Tagalog, 53
taga-ilog (tagalog), 4, 59
Tasadays, 7
Tausog natives, 12
Tydings-McDuffy Act, 16

U

United Farm Workers (labor
    union), 97, 103
Urdaneta, Andres, 8
utang naloob, 37, 60, 65, 66, 74
    (*see loob*)
utilitarianism, 106-108

V

values, 70, 73
values (Filipino), 101
visibility, 101

W

walang hiya, (see hiya)
women (Filipino), 54–54
worldview (Filipino), 49

Z

Zaide, G.P. (Filipino historian),
    128

About the Author

Dr. Romeo Solano Muñoz, a Filipino American emigrée, is a retired professor from the City Colleges of Chicago. He was on the faculty of Olive Harvey College in the Department of Learning Resources for 32 years, where he was Department Chair for a number of years. He retired in May, 2001. Dr. Muñoz is also active and a leader in the Filipino American community.

This book is the by-product of his doctoral dissertation, "A case study of Filipino American immigrants: invisibility, acculturation and adult learning," in Leadership and Educational Policy and Adult Learning at Northern Illinois University (DeKalb, Illinois). His first doctoral studies at Southern Illinois University (Carbondale, Illinois) were in Curriculum and Instruction and Instructional Technology administration.

Dr. Muñoz has been Deacon of the Catholic Archdiocese of Chicago for 26 years. He serves in the parish of St. Jude the Apostle (South Holland, Illinois) and an associate chaplain with the St. Jude Organization of the Chicago Police Department.

He lives in Chicago's south suburbs and is married to Soledad Roselado, a bilingual-bicultural educator. They have six children: Francis, Theresa, Romualdo (R-J), Cecilia, Anafe and Steve.